Practical Pointers For University Teachers

Bill Cox

**KOGAN
PAGE**

London ● Philadelphia

To my wife Pauline, my children Robert
and Martin and my mother, Gwen

First published in 1994

Apart from any fair dealing for the purposes of research or private study, or
criticism or review, as permitted under the Copyright, Designs and Patents Act,
1988, this publication may only be reproduced, stored or transmitted, in any form or
by any means, with the prior permission in writing of the publishers, or in the case
of reprographic reproduction in accordance with the terms of licences issued by the
Copyright Licensing Agency. Enquiries concerning reproduction outside those
terms should be sent to the publishers at the undermentioned address:

Kogan Page Limited
120 Pentonville Road
London N1 9JN

© Bill Cox, 1994

British Library Cataloguing in Publication Data

A CIP record for this book is available from the British Library.

ISBN 0 7494 1110 4

Typeset by DP Photosetting, Aylesbury, Bucks
Printed and bound in Great Britain by
Biddles Ltd, Guildford and King's Lynn

Contents

Acknowledgements

One of the great pleasures of writing this book has been the encouragement and support I have received from colleagues and friends, and the many discussions we have had. I would particularly like to mention: John Doidge and Pat Fleetwood-Walker for their initial encouragement to produce the book and for many comments on early drafts; Marlene Clayton, Bob Duggins, Barry Martin, George Paton, Phil Race, Anne Rushton, Hanifa Shah, and Dave Wilson for comments, information and corrections for the seemingly endless iterations of the manuscript; Lynn Burton for word-processing most of these, for finding me the right word or phrase when I didn't get it quite right, and for a first draft of the earlier sections of Chapter Six; Helen Carley, of Kogan Page, for her editorial assistance; and my wife Pauline for her patience, support and constructive criticism (of the book). To these, and many others, I would like to give my warm thanks. Also, I would like to thank Ron James, climber and teacher, who has always been an example to me of the difference a good teacher can make to those they teach.

Preface

This book evolved from guidelines provided for lecturers on Staff Development induction courses at Aston University. In writing the book, I didn't want to write a thesis on teaching, based on a particular philosophy, nor did I want to write a manual, or cookbook. Instead, I imagined that I was talking to a novice teacher, or an experienced colleague, and I told them what I felt they needed to think about, or what I thought about particular issues. The object is not to hand down advice or instruction. My aim is to provide pointers to assist readers in their own development as teachers through experience, further reading, discussion with their students and colleagues and their own reflections. I organized these pointers around Figure 1 (page 13) because this seemed to me to summarize the activities which we go through when preparing and delivering a course – it is basically how we do the job. I resisted – without great difficulty – the temptation to recast the result into erudite prose based on some teaching theme because (a) I wanted skim reading and dipping-in to be easy and (b) writing the book has robbed me of certainty about central themes of teaching. Indeed, having finished the book, I now feel that I am only just beginning to learn about teaching, and I can only invite you to join me.

I have also resisted the temptation to homogenize the style throughout: sometimes it is curt and functional and at others I go on a bit. If you talk to any experienced teacher for a few days, that is what you will get. Their advice on teaching will ebb and flow with mood and interest. It is easy to sanitize advice on teaching – expunge the opinion and idiosyncrasies – and leave the essential technicalities about boardwork, OHPs, etc. But there is much more to teaching than that, and I have tried to be as helpful as possible in regard to the job *as it is*. I hope that I have provided sufficient ideas and references for you to examine the pointers in further depth, and for you to form your own views, whether or not they coincide with mine.

BILL COX

Chapter One

Introduction

Aims and objectives

This book aims to provide university teachers with practical suggestions for efficient and effective teaching and assessment of students and evaluation of teaching quality. This covers such things as course planning and preparation, delivery and presentation, classroom management, student feedback and assessment, teaching quality evaluation and means of increasing teaching efficiency. I hope that the experienced teacher, as well as the newcomer, will find some things of interest, particularly in Chapters Six, Seven and Eight, which are devoted to accountability, efficiency and other teaching issues of our time which affect us all.

The book should help you to:

- prepare a given course within your expertise for a given number of students with a specified range of backgrounds and requirements;
- deliver the course effectively in the allotted time by a range of presentational techniques, maintaining a stimulating, structured and disciplined learning environment in the classroom, encouraging the learning process;
- maintain continuous assessment of student progress and provide appropriate feedback;
- assess students' competence and progress on completion of the course.
- contribute positively to evaluation of teaching quality on the course.
- critically examine and improve the efficiency of the teaching, while maintaining quality.

I won't attempt to provide a fully documented set of cut and dried rules for teaching 'correctly' – it does not exist. The idea is to present a reasonably organized and complete assembly of ideas and pointers, which will focus your own mind on the key issues and offer advice for your consideration. Some points are obvious imperatives, while others are more controversial. There may even be implicit contradictions. There will be personal prejudices and there will certainly be things with which you will disagree. These pointers may act as launch pads for debate with your students, or with colleagues, or for a deeper search of the literature. This is how we develop as teachers, not by reading a book.

There are many teaching skills which are common to most subject areas. These include course preparation commensurate with students' backgrounds and destinations; management of the teaching environment; use of teaching materials; communication and presentation skills; interpersonal skills; assessment. Further specific skills may be required for different subjects – for example, report marking in laboratory subjects. This book deals mainly with the general skills and relatively portable facets of subject-specific aspects, although I hope that points raised feed naturally into many subject-specific issues.

Apart from describing the technical aspects of teaching and its evaluation, this book also has a more general aim, which I think is almost as important these days. This relates to the moves to greater accountability and efficiency in teaching, dealt with in Chapters Six and Seven; and other issues such as the overloading of courses, the impact of new technology, and new managerial practices in universities, which are mentioned in Chapter Eight. There is no doubt that such developments have caught most academics, throughout the world, on the hop. Our response has ranged from piecemeal to panic. We have usually been too busy surviving to discuss or reflect on the changes sweeping over us. Certainly, coffee room talk has often revolved more around the latest government, institutional or managerial outrage, than on the teaching issues raised by all this. So one aim of this book is to encourage the university teaching profession to repossess these issues and retake the initiative.

Training and professional development

University teachers receive little or no training in teaching. It has simply been assumed, in most countries, that the highly qualified academic can easily master sufficient of the rudiments of teaching to satisfy most students, who are bright enough to study independently if need be, thereby marginalizing the importance of the teacher. Perhaps this is true. Maybe people are happy to pay to be taught by untrained teachers. But I wonder if they would fly with an airline with untrained pilots, or buy their house using an untrained solicitor. In fact, students in most developed countries regularly bemoan the lack of training their teachers receive. In Britain, the Students' Charter recommends that all teaching staff receive training in teaching. I think most university teachers would welcome this, if resources were made available. They are only too well aware that changes in curricula and teaching methods, wider access, increased accountability and efficiency, and new technology have found their traditional self-resourced, on-the-job training woefully inadequate.

Changes (good and bad) in society, government policy, technology, industry and commerce, are having their impact on university education.

Reduced funding will mean looking for more efficient means of teaching larger numbers of students. The mix of students may change, with increasingly heterogeneous backgrounds. The type of education demanded may change – more/less vocational; broader/narrower. The explosion of knowledge in all subjects may lead to even more specialization – or the need for a more portable, adaptable education. Advances in the theory of learning may influence teaching methods, as may improvements in information technology. These and other possibilities suggest that many changes and challenges lie ahead for university teachers and that we need to think deeply about our teaching and its methodology.

Many universities, particularly in the USA, Australia, New Zealand and Great Britain, now have staff development units which provide for some training in teaching, although often this is concentrated on new appointees. Diplomas, degrees and other awards in university teaching are beginning to emerge, some having a significant component of accredited prior learning, so that already established teachers may update and convert their skills into a formal qualification. An example of this is the new Master of Education for higher education teachers introduced at Sheffield University, England. There are also a number of centres specializing in university teaching around the world, developing, marshalling and disseminating good practice. In the Appendix I have given a brief description of some of the resources available to the university teacher who wishes to follow-up their interests in teaching, including journals, institutions and organizations.

Whether or not university teachers should be trained, they are jolly well going to be *assessed* and *appraised* on whatever it is that they need not be trained in. In Britain the Higher Education Quality Council is now charged with scrutinizing institutions' quality control mechanisms to ensure that they are satisfactory (*Quality Audit*), while the Higher Education Funding Council for England makes external judgement of the quality of teaching and learning in English institutions (*Quality Assessment*) (HEFCE, 1992). This may eventually come down to assessment of *your* teaching. Also, university teachers are now appraised annually, with teaching forming a significant component of the appraisal. In North America, evaluation of teaching has long been in place, with student rating of instruction being a major element, having an influence on promotion, tenure, salaries and advancement generally. So, in many countries university teachers are finding themselves increasingly accountable for their teaching. Whether or not this will make for better teaching depends crucially on how assessment and appraisal is conducted (Ramsden,1992). It will increase demand for good, well resourced training and professional development in teaching, which is no bad thing.

You as a teacher

You may have your own basic philosophy on education – how it should be conducted and funded. This will inevitably influence your approach and method in teaching and is worth some thought. For example, if you regard education as formal instruction by an expert to a motivated and con-scientious recipient, then you may incline towards traditional lecture methods. If you regard education as a shared collaborative exercise between adults, each tapping the others' talents and expertise, then you may favour a less formal group teaching approach. The important thing is not to let your personal preferences, attitudes and philosophy unduly influence your teaching to the extent that it compromises the teaching objectives.

Remember that the content and method of your teaching will also have to fit in with the policies of your institution and the requirements of the students and your colleagues. Other constraints will include financial resources, administrative and managerial considerations, classroom accommodation and so on. As well as having responsibilities to your colleagues and institution, you can also draw support and expertise from them. By far the most important advice anyone can give you is – consult widely with your colleagues on all teaching matters.

It is important to bear in mind that *you* were almost certainly not a typical student. You will have been selected precisely because of your exceptional academic qualities and your high level of motivation in your subject. (That is nice to hear, isn't it ?) Therefore, refrain from projecting your own ideas and attitudes on to your students, who may have completely different, no less worthy, abilities, interests and aspirations. Regard each as an individual and not necessarily as the sort of student you were.

Structure and organization of this book

The teaching profession is more complicated than most people appreciate and there is a bewildering array of teaching/learning activities which we perform in the academic year, not to mention our research and adminis-trative commitments. To make some sense of these and provide myself, if no one else, with a pattern for describing these activities and organizing my thoughts, I suggest Figure 1 as a schematic diagram of the teaching processes involved in giving a particular course. It also provides a frame-work on which to discuss such things as resourcing, evaluation of teaching quality, and efficiency. If you do not favour the scheme suggested, devise your own – the object is to establish a convenient framework around which to organize your thoughts.

Figure 1 provides a teacher-centred map of the activities we go through in the planning, preparation, presentation and assessment of a particular course. With minor modifications it could also be applied to a whole degree programme, or even to a single lecture or tutorial. The feedback loop illustrates development of the course in response to evaluation of the performance in each activity. Thus, given a course to teach we have to go through the following activities:

PLAN   the content and the teaching and assessment methods to be used.

PREPARE   the courseware, such as notes, exercises and problems, course guide, booklists, etc.; the assessment material to be used, and the course and teaching evaluation material required.

PRESENT   the course (sometimes in parallel with the preparation) deploying skills of delivery and classroom management.

ASSESS   the students, including possibly continuous assessment as well as a final examination requiring planning and preparation well in advance.

EVALUATE   the whole teaching process, possibly on a continuous, lecture by lecture basis, providing a feedback to course planning, development and preparation. Thus, particularly on first delivery of the course, you frequently need to use feedback from one lecture to help prepare the next.

The sub-headings under Preparation of Courseware refer to the broadly different types of teaching material we may have to produce – the course *notes*, material for student *activity*, such as problem sheets, and *supplementary* material such as reading lists. Again, if this division does not appeal to you, invent your own. It is broadly based on the idea that, one way or another, you will have to provide material which conveys the course content and supports your teaching activity; material which engages the students in learning activity, and various bits and pieces of administrative information.

The sub-headings under Teaching/Learning Activity refer to the broad

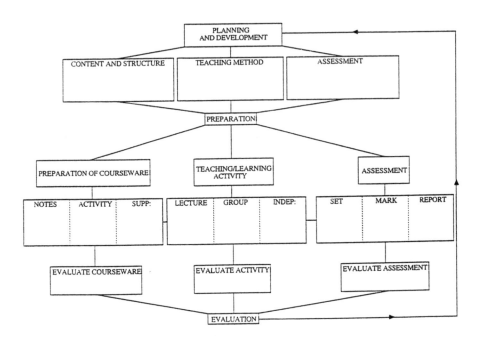

Figure 1   *The teaching activity*

types of teaching/learning activity in which you and the students become engaged – the 'formal' *lecture* or presentation by you to the students; the small *group* activity such as tutorials and seminars, which is essentially interactive; and the private *independent* study by students, which you may or may not structure. Again, this is subject-specific and a different break-down may be appropriate for you.

The sub-headings under Assessment are self explanatory – I have used *report* to refer to all aspects of end-use of the students' results, which may mean reporting to a formal Examination Board, or simply feedback to the students for teaching purposes.

This book will be structured according to Figure 1 although some of the activities inevitably overlap. In Chapter Two we consider the planning and development for a typical course. Chapter Three looks at the preparation of courseware suitable for a wide range of teaching methods. Chapter Four looks at all aspects of the teaching/learning activity, from formal lecturing to independent learning. Chapter Five discusses assessment, from formal examination to self-assessment. Regarding each of the frames on course-ware, teaching/learning activity and assessment as a continuum of teaching approaches, your own particular teaching activity through the course can be charted on the diagram.

Figure 1, or your version of it, can be used to organize your course documentation, whether hard copy or on computer. This includes the evaluation of the course and your teaching activity, so Chapter Six is structured around Figure 1. Our courses evolve each year as we find better ways of doing things and we continually evaluate and develop our teaching methods. But there may be a need for more formal, documented evaluation, providing concrete evidence of good teaching quality. This has long been the case in the USA . There is less of an ethos of accountability in teaching in mainland Europe, but every British academic must be aware of the recent moves towards quality audit and quality assessment in British universities. So, most university teachers throughout the world will now be invited to participate in some formal teaching evaluation process. Chapter Six looks at how the individual teacher might respond to this, and again uses Figure 1 as a framework for the discussion of such evaluation, identifying and relating all the various activities which may be evaluated, suggesting practical measures for doing this and for responding to the results.

There is no escaping the fact that many countries throughout the world are having to reduce their spending on all public services, including education. So there is increasing demand for efficiency in university teaching. Irrespective of one's feelings on this, the simple fact is that if our job is not to become unbearable, then we must either find ways of improving efficiency in all our teaching activities, or means of resisting the pressures to do so. In fact, careful thought on how we might do things more efficiently and improve our organization – personal, departmental and institutional – may be beneficial. Academics sometimes have something of a disdain for organization and efficiency, a legacy from more leisurely times when there were fewer students, adequate resources and a civilized regard for education. (Can anyone remember that now?) But these days careful organization and efficiency are becoming essential if we are to preserve our research time and not eat into social and family life. In Chapter Seven I discuss resourcing and possible efficiency gains against the framework of Figure 1, allowing us to compare different teaching strategies.

In Chapter Eight I open up some of the teaching issues raised by the sort of changes mentioned above. I certainly have no answers here. I would simply like more university teachers to start asking the questions.

Chapter Two

Planning and Development of a Course

Planning a course

The need for planning

Good planning is essential, from the overall degree programme, through specific courses, to individual lectures and other teaching activities. Also, courses should continually develop and evolve in response to evaluation of the strengths and weaknesses of content and delivery. Good teachers have always planned and developed their courses without the need for administrative jargon. Their expertise, intuition and discussion with colleagues usually sufficed and then they quickly got to work on preparation of the course. However, times have changed. Diminishing resources, increased student numbers and increased emphasis on the quality of teaching, mean that careful documented planning is now needed to operate with accountability within the increasing constraints on our flexibility and our budget.

The needs of planning

I'm concerned here with the planning required by the teacher when given a course for the first time. Broadly, within your resources, you have to decide on the content and structure of the course and devise appropriate teaching and assessment methods. You may also need to think about how you will evaluate the course and your teaching. Before you accept a course be sure that you can cope with the material, do justice to the students and effect the desired educational outcomes. You should also ensure that you have adequate preparation time, supporting resources, full information on the aims, goals and objectives of the course and on the students taking the course.

Find out as much as you can about the course by discussion with your colleagues, preferably the person who gave the course previously, if they have not already left (that may be the reason you are in the post!). Ideally, obtain a set of notes of the course, but do not feel bound to follow them rigidly. Consult past examination papers. If you feel the need, arrange for an adviser/mentor to be assigned to you – either by formally requesting this or informally latching on to a sympathetic and helpful colleague who has not got too many obvious prejudices.

Aspects of course planning

General curriculum planning – for example in the preparation of a new degree programme – is usually a joint effort, involving all of the contributing departments. The essentials of this may be thrashed out by a small working group, consulting all concerned parties and ratified by a university committee. The role of the individual teacher will usually be advisory, but everyone teaching on the programme needs to know the overall structure and the part their course plays in it. This Chapter is devoted to the planning and development of a single course, from its inception and design to the practical details of student contact.

When planning a course we need to ask:

- What is the **starting point** of the course (background of students, course prerequisites)?
- What **resources** are available for teaching the course?
- What are the **objectives** of the course (content and structure)?
- By what **teaching method** will the objectives be achieved?
- How will we **assess** achievement of the objectives (student assessment and feedback)?
- How will we **evaluate** the quality of the teaching?

The different aspects addressed by these questions cannot be considered in isolation. Planning and development of a course consists of a continual iteration through this list considering all aspects in parallel. For example, you may plan a particular teaching method to achieve a certain course objective, only to find that your resources will not run to it; so you may have to find an alternative method, or even drop that objective altogether. Thus, while the remaining sections of this chapter address these aspects of planning in turn, they are in fact all closely related.

Documentation

For some teachers (including myself) the idea of course documentation consists mainly of squeezing an increasing volume of notes, memos, coursework, examination papers and sundry paperwork into a bulging file, dreading the day we might actually have to retrieve something quickly. If we are truthful, this really is false economy. It does pay to keep your course documentation organized, readily accessible and regularly pruned. Indeed, any thorough assessment of teaching quality will place a high priority on good documentation of teaching and course materials, as this provides hard evidence of the quality, effectiveness and commitment of your teaching. How you organize and document your course material is very subjective and personal, but the sort of things it might include are:

- relation of the course to the rest of the curriculum;
- aims and objectives of the course;
- student records – including academic histories;
- timetable, including assessment deadlines;
- accommodation and teaching equipment, visual aids;
- staff support (shared tutorials, relevant tutors, etc.);
- syllabuses;
- teaching and learning methods used;
- methods of assessment;
- course notes;
- book lists;
- problem sheets;
- laboratory instructions;
- coursework;
- test, coursework, examination marks;
- destination of students;
- relevant performance indicators;
- any developments, novel features, displaying innovation in teaching;
- student questionnaires and other course evaluation material.

Starting point

Differences in background and motivation

For some courses this is the most difficult aspect of planning. You must start from a position accessible to the students. For, say, a third-year course where the preparation and prerequisites have been provided in-house, you will have a fair idea of the background of the students and therefore where to start. However, modularization and credit transfer schemes of various kinds, between and within institutions, can still result in some uncertainty about the background of students and their degree of preparation. Perhaps more important, if your course is inter-disciplinary, is the difference in nature and levels of motivation between students from different disciplines. Since an important task in the early stages of a course is to provide motivation, you may need to consider how best to do this with a group with disparate interests.

Such considerations are even more important in the case of first-year courses, where the entry is usually direct from school. In Britain, the USA and many other countries there has been a move towards broadening the school curriculum in the last decade. The result is that the academic background of university entrants has become more heterogeneous, and putative means of assessing competence (such as A-levels in Britain) are now very unreliable in some subjects. Planning first-year courses must therefore address the problem of 'bringing the students up to standard'. Also, the modern schoolchild is often used to a teaching method (more practical, interactive, student-centred, a greater emphasis on transferable skills) different from the formal approach traditional in universities. Thus, the transition from school to university, both in knowledge base and attitudes, now extends well into the first year and needs to be well planned, possibly requiring a different approach from that appropriate in subsequent years.

Review and revision

Planning the starting point will therefore require research into the background of your students. You may need to plan some diagnostic testing, to review the range and level of their skills, and to supplement this with flexible revision material to consolidate these skills. Also, you may need to consider training in study skills or learning activity which may be new to the students. The aim is to start the bulk of the students off from roughly the same point, so that not too many are lost because it is too hard or bored because it is too easy. Diminishing resources have severely constrained our options here – streaming, remedial classes, additional personal tuition are all becoming expensive luxuries.

Information on the background of the students on your course may come from many sources and you need to be aware of the limitations of this information. Pay particular attention to non-standard qualifications and try to translate these into reliable information about the knowledge base of the students. Remember that the point you must start from is not what you think they ought to know, nor what you think they know, but *what you know they know*.

Resources

You

You are the main resource for any course you teach. This includes your expertise and your time. By 'expertise' I don't mean your subject expertise alone. Some of the worst teachers are those who know their subject inside out but are unable to teach that knowledge to the students, with all their various backgrounds and motivations. You must know your subject, of course, but you must also know how to teach it – a different thing altogether. Your time means more than purely class contact time. It includes preparation, student consultation, examination invigilation, marking, sundry meetings connected with the course and the tiresome associated administration – that is a lot of time. Therefore, at the risk of labouring the obvious, don't rush to take on that extra course, even if it seems attractive to you! The highest resource priority in the planning of the course is that you are an adequate resource.

Secretarial, administrative and technical support

Good support staff are invaluable. Your job is to teach, do research and dispose of administration as painlessly as possible. There is so much which support staff can do to help you in this and, like you, the better they are treated, the better they will perform. So, get your work to them in good time, involve them in what you are doing, be sure that they can cope with the workload which your planning involves and encourage and reward their initiative and imagination. With the advent of word processors there is a growing tendency for academic staff to become their own secretaries. Up to a point there are some things teachers may do for themselves more efficiently than enlisting the help of support staff. But, on the whole, if you are doing something your secretary could be doing, you are operating inefficiently, and if your institution is under-resourcing you to the extent that you are performing secretarial tasks, then it is operating inefficiently. Transfer as much of your work as possible to your support staff.

Print-based materials

Within reason such things as stationery, photocopying, printing facilities and so on are relatively inexpensive resources. However, if you are producing comprehensive printed notes as handouts to large classes, then the cost can be significant and you need to ensure that your resources are adequate for this. You must also allow time for preparation of such materials. And beware of busy times of the year, such as the beginning of term and examination times. Be prepared for a queue at the photocopier!

Classroom accommodation and equipment

Someone, somewhere, in your institution will have responsibility for assigning your lectures and tutorials to specific rooms with particular facilities. Find out who it is – you will very likely have to contact them before the year is out. Also, if your planned teaching method requires dedicated accommodation or equipment, such as projection facilities, then you must see that this is provided, in good time. For large lectures you may need a tiered lecture theatre; for seminars a small room with flexible seating arrangement may be more appropriate. Your planning must take such things into account. An extreme example of the need for careful long-term planning of accommodation and equipment requirements would arise if you intended to introduce an element of computer-assisted learning into your course.

Library facilities

Whether you give directed reading, have a set course book, or simply issue a list of useful titles should the students require additional reading, ensure that your library has the resources needed by the students. If the students are required to purchase a book, alert the local bookshop. Take particular care with large classes. If you plan to use directed reading coupled with continuous assessment, then be sure this will not overstretch library resources.

No resources, no courses

These days, and for the foreseeable future, you will not find resources for teaching easy to come by, no matter where you teach. Most institutions, throughout the world, are suffering real and significant cuts in their income, and neither you nor the students can be sheltered from this. Nor is it practical, in the short term, to attack governments, university leadership or anyone else for the situation – this is the job of teachers' leaders and representatives, and all we can do is inform, encourage and support them. In the meantime, as individuals we must fight for our due resources to do our job of teaching. At the same time we must not undermine the collegial structure which is so essential in all education, and so we must not fall into the trap of fighting each other for the meagre resources available. We must make the case for our teaching resources with reasonableness, and with the same detached objectivity that we (are supposed to) bring to our research or other scholarly activities. And we must give the cases made by others the same objective consideration. However, while adopting a spirit of compromise, their are limits below which allocated resources are inadequate to support the quality of education the students are entitled to expect. That is where you draw the line – no resources, no courses. Enlist the support of your students, your colleagues, your professional association, external bodies, relevant legislation (if there is any left), and anyone else who will listen, to ensure that you have at least the minimum resources to do your job efficiently and effectively. And if you don't get the minimum resources, refuse to teach the course.

Objectives and structure

The importance of objectives

A clearly defined set of educational and subject-specific objectives is essential for course planning and will influence your choice of included topics and the time allocated to each. It will also bear on the teaching methods you use, and particularly on the assessment procedure – it is not easy to set an examination paper unless you know what the students are supposed to have learnt. Objectives should be matched to the students' background, appropriate teaching and learning activities and the form of the assessment. Also, remember that when informing your students of the course objectives, these need to be expressed in such a way that the student, as yet untutored in the subject, can at least gain an appreciation of what is intended – so use as little jargon as possible. On the other hand there is a view, particularly in arts subjects, that rigid, prescribed objectives are too restrictive and stultifying. This may be so, and perhaps all that the teacher can then say is how they expect the students to be changed by the course, giving rather broader attitudinal objectives.

Content of the course

By 'content' I mean all aspects of knowledge, skills and attitudes which we wish to impart and also the intellectual experiences of all involved in the course – thus, assessment would be regarded as course content, particularly if it is continuous assessment. The content will emerge naturally from your educational and subject-specific objectives. Much of the course content may be prescribed by the overall programme structure. However, you will always have a little latitude in defining detailed subject-specific objectives and therefore some freedom over the course content.

Sharing objectives with the students

Some people favour allowing students to formulate their own objectives. In practice, in many subjects the students have neither the experience nor expertise to do this, can rarely agree among themselves and prefer objectives laid down by the teacher, department or institution. Besides, they would be deprived of the pleasure of criticising the course if they were responsible for producing it.

However, there are a number of ways in which the students may be involved in the planning, preparation and conduct of their course. At the start of the course you may find it worthwhile to establish a 'learning contract' with your students (Stephenson and Laycock, 1993). You may do this with the whole class, coming to some agreement on the structure and emphasis of the course and possibly its content to some extent. This may also include some agreement on methods of teaching/learning and assessment. Some people go so far as agreeing written contracts with individual students, allowing them to negotiate the content and assessment procedure to match their particular needs and strengths. Clearly, this involves the teacher in a great deal of work and is perhaps too formal for some tastes. It certainly requires careful planning.

It is, however, essential that the objectives are shared with the students. The aims and objectives of the course must be made explicit to the students, so that they know what is expected of them – and, more prosaically, what they will be examined on. Objectives are perhaps best expressed in terms of what the students should be able to do on completion of the course. Also, the students like to know what they can expect from you. This includes such things as your depth of treatment, the standards you expect, your availability for consultation, and so on. These rather subjective things are often of the most interest to students, giving them a feel for the severity of your course.

Educational objectives

One widely accepted classification of educational objectives is that proposed by Bloom (1956), who argued that a course should equip students to:

RECALL AND RECOGNIZE specified information.
COMPREHEND and digest the information.
APPLY what they have learned.
ANALYSE the subject, with an understanding of the component parts and their interrelationships.
SYNTHESIZE the subject, taking an overview.
EVALUATE their knowledge, understanding and competence critically.

Bloom's taxonomy has, if nothing else, promoted healthy controversy in the literature (Dressel, 1976) and I don't offer it as gospel. It is best to regard such theoretically based material as simply one component of advice you take on developing your teaching, and balance it carefully against other sources such as colleagues, students and sheer common sense. Gurus and slavish adoption of any particular theory have no place in teaching (or any other enlightened activity for that matter).

Educational objectives may be broadly classified as based on knowledge, skills, or attitude. Bloom's list is usually regarded as being concerned with knowledge-based objectives, where the main emphasis is on recall of information, understanding of concepts and problem-solving processes. Skills objectives are less easily characterized, since the degree of proficiency required is more difficult to quantify – for example, both solicitors and barristers require skills in presenting a case, but of a somewhat different order. Attitudinal objectives are even more difficult to categorise and much more contentious. Thus, we may have particular professional attitudes which we wish to instil, which are perceived to be desirable at the present time – but how do we know we are not perpetuating inappropriate attitudes, stultifying the development of the subject? Also, to what extent are the attitudes influenced by cultural and other prejudices? Dressel (1976) gives a good treatment of the classification of educational objectives and its pitfalls.

Subject objectives

Key questions from which subject objectives will emerge include:

- How does the course relate to the rest of the curriculum?
- What are the prerequisites for the course?
- What does the student/department/university expect of the course?
- What is the academic background of the students enrolled on the course – do they meet the prerequisites of the course; if not, what are the deficiencies?
- With what essential knowledge/concepts/skills/attitudes must the course equip the student?
- What teaching methods and materials are appropriate?
- How do you intend to assess the students?

As an exercise, you might like to consider these questions in the context of one of your own courses.

The objectives will guide you to the content of the course, resulting in a list of topics you need to cover and an idea of what to teach on each topic. Prioritize these topics. Some will be essential – other courses may rely on you to cover them. Textbooks and colleagues will provide a guide to what constitutes the main body of knowledge appropriate to the level, duration and context of the course and this may fix a large proportion of your content. Then you may have some freedom to introduce less essential topics and a few choice morsels which you particularly relish. Don't be afraid to include pet topics of your own – the students rarely share your enthusiasm, but they often do react positively to it. You may also need to include revision topics required to level out the background of the students – these may be an essential component of the course, even though they may not be directly examinable.

The most usual outcome of the specifications of the course objectives is a *syllabus*, itemizing those topics the course will cover, indicating knowledge, skills and attitudes which one wishes to impart and quantifiers of the extent to which the material will be covered. This should be more than the half-page list of topic headings that many of us have come to confuse with a syllabus. It should really list the subject-specific objectives at some length. A standard format for stating objectives takes the form 'At the end of the course you should be able to ...'

Other factors affecting course content

The choice of topics, relations between them and the depth of treatment may also be constrained by other considerations (Newble and Cannon, 1991):

PHILOSOPHICAL	–	depth or breadth? vocational or pleasure?
PROFESSIONAL	–	accreditation requirements; ethical matters.
PSYCHOLOGICAL	–	requirement to enhance and facilitate the learning process.
PRACTICAL	–	resources; access to library; availability of equipment.
STUDENT	–	needs and abilities of students.

You will also need to consider the requirements of your colleagues and the institution. Further, the external funding bodies may have indirect influence on your choice of subject matter – for example, there may be pressures to make courses more 'relevant' or vocational. The important thing is to identify all factors which influence the content of the course and then accommodate them as best you can.

Transferable skills

It may be desirable to provide training in appropriate *transferable skills* in your course. These are portable skills which can be used across a wide range of disciplines, in many activities and environments and which may be developed in any particular subject. They include communication, inter-personal, quantification, analytical, synthesis, problem solving and evaluation skills. Many employers place higher value on these skills than they do on the specific subject matter of a student's degree. Training in such skills usually requires a particular type of teaching/learning method (for example oral presentation, project work, report writing, role play).

Special needs

You may have to consider students with special needs or characteristics which may influence your choice or treatment of topics. Examples include mature students, handicapped students, overseas students, students with unusual or deficient backgrounds, etc. Newble and Cannon (1991) give a number of examples of the ways in which teachers need to accommodate such special groups.

Don't cover too much

Be realistic about the number and range of topics you include. Better a smaller number of topics treated more thoroughly than skimping through too many. Also, when looking at the official time available for the course, remember that you will inevitably lose some of this, so allow some slack in the amount of material you attempt to cover.

Structure of the course

Having decided, albeit approximately, the content of the course, organize the topics into a sequence suitable for presentation to the students. There will not be a unique way to do this but there are some useful general guidelines and suggestions worth noting. We obviously need to start from the students' present level of understanding and build on that. It is some-times best to work from the specific to the general, abstracting general principles from easily accessible relevant examples. We might follow the historical development of the subject, or it might lend itself to a particularly transparent logical development. We can group topics around important themes, concepts or problems. Another direction we can take is to start from a particularly complex situation and prune and simplify until we get to an understanding of the essential underlying principles. Again, there will be plenty of advice on this from textbooks and colleagues, and much will be automatically prescribed by the serial nature of most subjects. The organi-zation and sequencing of topics will also be influenced by your educational objectives (Bligh *et al.*, 1981; Rowntree, 1981). Other useful suggestions include:

- Alternate boring topics with interesting ones.
- Allow more time for tougher topics and adapt teaching methods accordingly.
- Arrange topics so as to bring out their role in the overall structure.
- Allocate time to topics in proportion to their importance.

Both for your own use in planning and for the students' benefit in your presentation make imaginative use of diagrams, flowcharts or other pictorial representations (such as Figure 1), illustrating the structure of the course and linkages between and within topics in the course. Simply trying to draw such diagrams helps you to sort out your ideas and provides the students with a logical plan to follow.

Courseware

Once you have an idea of the content and structure of your course, and the resources available, then you can plan the preparation of the teaching materials or *courseware* which you will need. This includes everything required in the presentation of the course, either for your own use or for issue to the students. The courseware you require will depend on the course objectives, your teaching methods, and will be constrained by your resources (Ellington and Race, 1993).

Planning teaching methods/learning activities

Methods, objectives, resources – the right balance

Early in the planning stage you will need to think about the teaching/learning activity. What sort of teaching methods are you going to use; what are the students going to be doing? The main educational principle which should be your guide here is that your methods and the student activity must be such as to achieve the course objectives efficiently and effectively. Usually this will mean that you cannot use the most appropriate method/activity for *all* your objectives – you have a problem of constrained optimization. If you feel that your resources and your course objectives constrain you to a pattern of teaching/learning activities which is an inappropriate match to the objectives, then you must negotiate additional resources, or an alternative set of objectives. This aspect of planning is becoming particularly relevant as resources for teaching are reduced. Options for efficiency, dealt with in Chapter Seven, include assigning more directed reading, sitting the students in front of a computer, showing them a video, or booking them into the Albert Hall. But all these compromise some educational objectives and therefore require careful thought and planning.

The 'standard' method

Teaching is an ancient craft. Humans have used 'teaching methods' since Adam and Eve taught their offspring to walk – and I've no doubt they argued about the best way to do that! Yet, it is still impossible to lay down 'the best way to teach'. I'm certainly not going to attempt that. In your particular subject there will be a wealth of expertise, wisdom, tradition, custom and practice for you to tap. My guess is that in most cases you will find the standard teaching method is the 'formal' lecture, supplemented with tutorials, discussion groups or laboratory classes. Such an approach is flexible, economical, easy to plan and is probably as effective as most.

Active learning

To many teachers the conventional formal lecture is restrictive and uninspiring, and they prefer a more activity based presentation, splitting it up into short formal sessions separated by directed learning activities designed to motivate and maintain interest and arousal. Usually such *active learning* requires (at least initially) more careful planning than the formal lecture format, and possibly more resources. Many teachers would like to teach this way, given time and resources, but most of us tend to compromise by livening up our lectures with a few questions, setting some simple exercises, or encouraging (brief) discussion. Active learning methods form the basis of a series of modules on effective teaching produced by the UK's Universities' Staff Development Unit (USDU) of the Committee of Vice Chancellors and Principals (CVCP) based at Sheffield University (CVCP/USDU, 1992; see also Habeshaw, 1989; Gibbs and Jenkins, 1992 and Race and Brown, 1993).

Independent learning

There is a current fashion to encourage *independent learning* in students, driven more by cynical resource motives than respectable educational motives, one suspects. This approach goes under a number of names, such as open learning, self instruction, individualized instruction. Essentially they all amount to a redistribution of the time spent by the student in the various learning activities they undertake in their study for the course. Depending on the proportion of the degree programme that it represents, you can only expect students to spend a certain number of hours per week on your course, including contact and private study time. The key question is how is that time to be divided up between teaching/learning activities? Experienced teachers all have their own rule of thumb. I assume that for every contact hour my students will put in at least two hours work in their own time. I hope that with this sort of commitment the average student will cope quite well with the course. Open learning looks more carefully at such a distribution of time. Perhaps, with sufficiently supportive courseware, I could forego some of the contact time, leaving the students to study for themselves (after all, the British Open University and all correspondence schools rely almost entirely on this). There are clearly many interesting possibilities here, but again requiring considerably more planning and resources than for the 'standard' method. Good introductions to open learning methods include the books by Race (1989) and Rowntree (1990).

Matching methods to objectives

Your teaching methods/learning activities should be matched to the objectives of the course. An example here is the teaching of an experimental subject where some topics of a theoretical nature are best covered by formal lectures, while others demand hands-on experience in the laboratory. But there are more subtle examples – for instance, having just expounded at length on a particularly difficult conceptual point, in formal lecture mode, you may be moving on to some routine material, which you can best cover by allowing the students a 10-minute work session on simple examples. Or, you might have a suitable activity to reinforce the difficult conceptual point. A session on the computer may be appropriate for one topic, a video for another. A handout may work best for this topic, straight chalk and talk with note-taking is better for that. Flexibility is the key. When informing the students of the course objectives you might also describe the associated teaching/learning activities.

Types of teaching/learning activity

There are many types of teaching/learning activity for you to choose from, bearing in mind appropriateness to objectives, size of group, resources, accommodation, effectiveness, and other considerations. Some of the most common are listed below.

- FORMAL LECTURE
  Virtually uninterrupted monologue taking occasional questions. Almost an address. 'Chalk and talk'. Can be used for any size of group. Tiered lecture room preferable if the class is large.
- ACTIVE LECTURE
  Lecture period including mini-sessions of student activity. May involve brainstorming, buzz groups, case studies, discussion, demonstrations and other interactive teaching methods. Works better with small to medium groups but may be used for large groups with careful planning and suitable accommodation. Preferably flat room and flexible seating arrangement.
- TUTORIAL/EXERCISE CLASS
  Students work through set problems, individually or together, with assistance as necessary from tutor. Best in groups of less than 30. Flat spacious room for ease of access and flexible seating plan.
- SEMINAR
  Presentation of a piece of prepared work by a student to his/her peers and subsequent discussion roughly structured by the tutor. No more than a dozen students. Cosy flat room with suitable seating plan.
- ROLE PLAY/GAMES
  Students act out roles or play games for the purpose of learning and developing specific skills. Very small to small groups. May need dedicated accommodation and equipment.
- LABORATORY CLASSES
  For practical sessions required in experimental subjects or languages. Specially designed laboratories required, and these determine the size of the group.

- PERSONAL TUTORING

  One-to-one discussion of students' work and problems with a tutor (in some institutions this would be called a tutorial). Tutor's office (or the pub).

- OPEN LEARNING (OR INDEPENDENT LEARNING)

  The students effectively teach themselves with the support of specially prepared courseware, frequent monitoring and feedback and maybe a small number of classroom sessions. Number and accommodation not really relevant except for assessment purposes – which is why the method has been seized upon by those demanding greater efficiency in teaching.

- PEER TUTORING

  The students teach each other, within a structured format provided by the tutor, so that it does not degenerate to the blind leading the blind. Small groups (half-dozen) with suitable seating plan. Very effective in training in the use of equipment such as computers, where students have a natural tendency to help each other out.

- PRIVATE STUDY

  What (we hope) the students do in their own time, complementing the contact time – maybe reading their notes or working through problems. The tutor can still influence this by timetabling set work, for example.

- COMPUTER ASSISTED LEARNING

  Students use dedicated teaching software, the best of which is interactive and (moderately) intelligent, to learn some of the course material. Computing laboratories or personal computer required – extremely expensive, in capital expenditure, maintenance and renewal, and staff time.

Teaching methods are discussed further in Chapter Three.

The preferred teaching method may differ for different subjects. For example, formal lectures are often favoured in science and engineering subjects, whereas discussion groups tend to be more appropriate in arts and social studies subjects. Class sizes will influence the teaching method, the informal interactive approach suitable for small group tutorials being difficult to maintain in a very large lecture class, for example. Also different approaches may be needed for different levels of course. Thus, final-year classes are usually relatively straightforward to teach, as you can often rely on a high level of independence and motivation, while first-year elementary inter-disciplinary classes are often the most difficult, requiring mature and sympathetic teaching.

Planning assessment of students

Assessment requires early planning

Even if you intend to assess the students only by an examination at the end of the course – maybe nine months away – you still need to plan it well ahead. If you decide on an element of continuous assessment then this must be timetabled in parallel with your presentation of the course. Setting assessment is one of the easiest things to underestimate in preparing a course, particularly if you are new to the game. Whatever assessment method you decide to use, it must be a valid and reliable test of achievement of the course objectives, and to ensure this you need to be thinking about it right from the beginning of your course planning.

Matching assessment to objectives

Assessment, like your teaching methods, must be matched to your course objectives – much of the students' time is spent trying to do this in great detail – 'will we need this for the examination?' being one question students *can* be relied upon to ask. For example, if you require only a superficial knowledge of some topic, which you conveyed by showing a video, then any examination question must reflect that – the students will be understandably miffed if they are suddenly faced with an intricate in-depth question on the topic, requiring detailed knowledge. Thus, when planning your assessment (which may, of course, be other than a written examination), check that it is consistent with your stated objectives.

Self-, peer- and group-assessment

It may be appropriate for some subjects/purposes to introduce an element of self-assessment. For example, you may wish to develop students' self-critical capabilities. This requires considerably more planning than even continuous assessment. Part of your planning will need to include consideration of the training needs of the students and yourself in self-assessment methods. The same might be said about peer-assessment and group-assessment. While such methods are useful means of assessing the skills required in team-work, for example, they require careful planning, again including the training of the students and yourself.

Evaluation and development

Evaluation

When evaluating the quality of a course and its teaching, we first look at the course content and structure in relation to the rest of the curriculum, and the extent to which it achieves the educational and subject objectives. This is often the job of a departmental or university committee, to which you simply provide input on request. Then there is the evaluation of the actual teaching/learning process, monitoring the components of Figure 1. This may be largely your responsibility, and you will need to think about how to do it efficiently and effectively. This is the subject of Chapter Six. You will need to plan your method of evaluating the various aspects of the teaching (questionnaire, student interviews, classroom observation), your timetable for doing this, and the time and resources you will need.

Information for evaluation of a course and its teaching comes from many sources, internal and external to the institution. For example, evaluation evidence may be provided by yourself, students, colleagues, university committees and review groups, previous graduates, external examiners, employers, professional associations and educational experts. Also, your courseware and other documentation, such as results of assessment and reports of course review committees, provide valuable information. Tapping all these sources is probably impractical for most of us, so we have to choose those which are most cost effective.

The evaluation evidence may be collected in many ways – student questionnaires and interviews, discussion with colleagues, diaries and work records, checklists, written submissions and testimonials, classroom observation, making audio or video recording of lessons, assessment results, library and laboratory usage statistics, and reports of external examiners. And don't forget that the simplest, most common and *possibly* most effective means of collecting evidence are informal discussion with students and colleagues, monitoring of coursework and discussions at examination boards. However, we will increasingly be expected to provide formal documentation of evaluation, and so we each need to design a practical and effective evaluation strategy, within our means. See Chapter Six, page 99, for some ideas about doing this.

Development

The *development* of a course, by the continual updating and improvement of its content, structure and teaching, takes place almost on a day to day basis, in response to the on-going evaluation of the processes involved and out-comes achieved. Some development will be led by a departmental or university committee, and will require little more from you than the implementation of any agreed changes. In other cases you may feel the need for a major revision of your teaching methods or the course structure, involving you in significant planning. As a general rule note that evaluation and development are really inseparable – you cannot develop your course without evaluation, and there is little point in evaluation if you are not going to act on it.

Chapter Three

Preparation of Courseware

A model

The need for good preparation

The amount of courseware you will need to prepare depends on your chosen teaching method, but in any event good preparation, as early as possible, is one of the musts of effective teaching. The preparation may already be there, in your head, if you are thoroughly familiar with the subject and can lecture off the cuff – but nevertheless, even the individual lecture requires forethought and preparation. If your courseware is so good that students can all but do without you, then you can relax and spend your contact time guiding the students and encouraging independent study, without having to wade through routine aspects.

Be thorough and professional in your preparation. This will give you confidence in the classroom. A teacher's lack of preparation is easily spotted by the students, who can be merciless in drawing attention to it. Whereas an experienced teacher can sometimes cope by staying one week ahead of the students, the novice really needs to be well ahead to have the desired overview and awareness of the tricky areas. Questioning students to obtain their views on the characteristics of poor lecturing, I have been struck by the number of references to poor preparation and consequent erratic and hesitant delivery.

Steps to preparing courseware

Preparation of course material is a very personal activity. Two equally effective teachers may have entirely different approaches. In Figure 2 I suggest a working model comprising the main components of courseware preparation, which are probably implicitly used by most of us. Again, if this scheme is not to your taste, adapt it to suit your individual needs. Essentially, you have to convey the course content by providing the students with a good set of notes or the equivalent; you have to give them something to do

THE COMPONENTS OF COURSEWARE PREPARATION :-

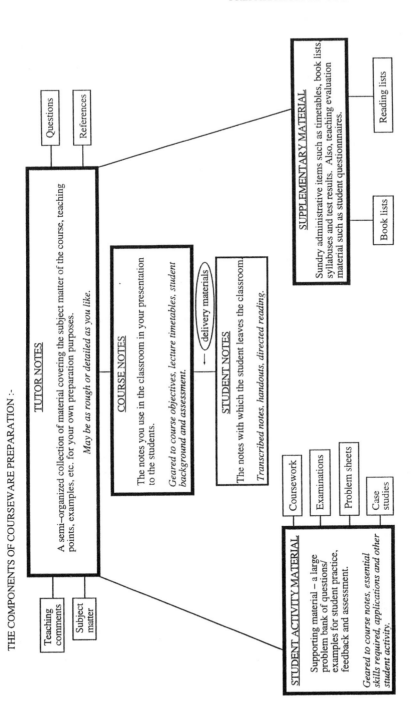

TUTOR NOTES

A semi-organized collection of material covering the subject matter of the course, teaching points, examples, etc. for your own preparation purposes.

May be as rough or detailed as you like.

Questions

References

Teaching comments

Subject matter

COURSE NOTES

The notes you use in the classroom in your presentation to the students.

Geared to course objectives, lecture timetables, student background and assessment.

delivery materials

STUDENT NOTES

The notes with which the student leaves the classroom.

Transcribed notes, handouts, directed reading.

SUPPLEMENTARY MATERIAL

Sundry administrative items such as timetables, book lists, syllabuses and test results. Also, teaching evaluation material such as student questionnaires.

Book lists

Reading lists

STUDENT ACTIVITY MATERIAL

Supporting material – a large problem bank of questions/ examples for student practice, feedback and assessment.

Geared to course notes, essential skills required, applications and other student activity.

Coursework

Examinations

Problem sheets

Case studies

Figure 2 *Preparation of courseware*

to practise and test their knowledge and skills, and you also need to provide them with various items of administrative information.

Your notes and the students' notes

In planning the course you will have gained a rough idea of what you hope to cover and will be able to gather together the basic notes on subject matter, teaching points, problems to set the students, and so on. I call these the *tutor's notes*. They are personal to the tutor and may be a very ramshackle affair – from a few brief outline notes to well thumbed dog-eared remnants of previous years' notes. From these you can prepare a more polished set of notes – the *course notes* – which you use in your presentation to the students. These may simply be the same as your tutor notes, but in practice your tutor notes may include all manner of peripheral material and it is safest if your course notes bear a close relation to what the students actually receive – the *student's notes*. The latter are literally what the student walks out of the classroom with. If you use chalk and talk or overhead projector (OHP) for your delivery, the student's notes will consist of what they have managed to transcribe from your presentation. They may be identical to your course notes, particularly if you use comprehensive handouts. I hope my distinction between tutor's notes, course notes and student's notes does not seem pedantic. It is my attempt to emphasize that in courseware preparation we have to identify what it is that we wish to convey to the students (tutor's notes), decide how we will transmit it (course notes), and anticipate what they will receive as a result (student's notes).

If you are using open/active learning methods then your course notes may consist of highly structured support material including motivational exercises, detailed explanations, work timetables, study guide, self-assessment facilities and directions for activities. The result may be a self-contained coursebook encompassing all teaching material and virtually rendering you redundant (which may be your objective, of course).

The transfer from your course notes to the student's notes is a crucial stage in the teaching process. Particularly if you are using chalk and talk, the quality of the student's notes depends a great deal on your classroom and teaching skills, and on the student's skills at note taking. In practice, the student's notes form the foundation for his or her study of the course. The lectures or other contact sessions usually provide only the skeleton of the subject matter, and most students rely heavily on their personal notes to consolidate this in their own time at their own pace (which is why they like comprehensive printed notes). Sending the students out with a good set of notes is half the battle won, the lecture having primed them for the material they have received, guiding them through the highlights and hurdles.

Student activity material

From your tutor's notes you may also prepare additional material such as worksheets and reading lists. Most important are the problems or exercises which you use for student practice, feedback and assessment, which we might call the student *activity* material. Your course notes only provide the raw material for the student to work on. Most of the students' learning is then done by working through problems or practical sessions, repeatedly practising the skills they have acquired. On completion of this process, the most effective means of assessing their progress is by setting them further problems. You may find it useful to collate a large set of problems, with a wide range of difficulty, into a *problem bank*, which you can build up during your course preparation. You can then dip into this to prepare tutorial material, exercise sheets, coursework problems and examination questions.

Supplementary material

You will also need to prepare sundry supplementary material such as syllabus, book lists, reading lists, timetables and other information not already included in your course notes or activity material. It is *particularly* important to give a written statement of precisely how the students will be assessed on your course and not to leave it to someone else to tell them – they never do! Also, you may need some material for evaluating your teaching or the course in general. This might include student questionnaires, for example. Evaluation material is discussed in Chapter Six.

Minority and special needs

When preparing courseware, give some thought to any minority or special-needs groups in your class, such as mature or overseas students, or to those with non-standard qualifications. You may be able to help them cope better with your course by appropriate preparation of the teaching material. For example, keeping the English simple will help foreign students.

Types of courseware

The sort of courseware you need to provide for the student, one way or another, may include:

Syllabus	Assessment information
Weekly timetable of topics	Examination schedule
Course notes	Examination papers
Problem sheets	Project specifications
Reading lists	Audio cassettes
Coursework	Video material
Worked examples	Experiment specifications
Specimen examination paper	Case study notes
Revision material	Computer software
Tests	Student questionnaires

In each case, you must consider preparation time, resources and relevant departmental or institutional policy.

Basic principles

Whenever you are preparing courseware there are a number of basic principles which you should bear in mind (Newble and Cannon, 1991).

- It should be relevant and appropriate to the students' level of understanding of the topic.
- Its relation to the teaching and learning activities of the course should be clear.
- It should be as simple and uncomplicated as possible, consistent with the message it is intended to convey.
- Emphatic signals such as underlining or use of colours should be used to maximum effect to stress important points.
- It is a good idea to adopt a consistent personal style for your courseware.

Also, if possible, put your courseware on floppy disc, for ease of editing, portability, and dissemination. This also aids in composing the text for your course notes. Thank heavens for word processors when it comes to systematically constructing a finished piece of writing from an initial rough draft.

Preparation takes time

Estimate how much time you will need for preparation – then treble it. You will be amazed at how much time it takes to produce a couple of pages of notes on even an elementary topic. Where do you start? What exactly is it you want to say? How best to express it? When is an example appropriate? A survey of my colleagues produced estimates of 4–10 hours preparation for a one-hour lecture for first delivery of a course. If you are new to teaching, work on the 10 hours. On the other hand, it is sometimes a mistake to put too much effort into preparing the notes. There is something to be said for leaving your preparation until the last possible moment – many people work best and produce their most succinct material when panic stricken!

Packaged teaching

Provided you have the resources (and are sufficiently organized) you may find it useful to collect all your courseware in a work-book or teaching package issued to the students at the beginning of your course. This saves tedious weekly distribution and allows the students to work ahead if they wish. Also, of course, there is the possibility that you may never see the students again until the examination.

Tutor's and course notes

Your starting point

You will rarely have to prepare your course totally from scratch. Thus, you may inherit a set of notes, or a suggested course text on which to base your material and you can use these to a greater or lesser extent, depending on the preparation time available to you. If time is pressing and you are comfortable with the idea, there is no great harm in leaning heavily on such readily available material, in the first presentation at least. But try to evolve your own individual set of notes as soon as possible to put your own stamp on the course. If you are not happy with using prior material in this way and wish to develop your own from scratch, then you will need more preparation time and you are entitled to insist on this. The rest of this section covers preparation from scratch and you can short-cut the process depending on material available to you.

Tutor's rough notes

You might first prepare a set of rough outline notes which do little more than provide a summary of what you must cover to achieve the course objectives. These may consist simply of lists of key points such as concepts, definitions, techniques, theorems and proofs. As you accumulate these, by consulting books or colleagues, various ideas on their role in the course and on their presentation will occur to you – jot these down, too. Also, questions will occur to you – make a note of these as they are also likely to occur to the student, or you may be able to use them on problem sheets, for example.

This process, resulting in pages of scribbled comments, ideas, questions and key points, may just as well be done quickly (this book started life as a couple of dozen such pages of jottings, during a few wet days in the Lake District). You may have forgotten some things and you may have many points you will later jettison, but that doesn't matter, your list will provide a rough basis for getting an overview of the material and then you can start organizing it and producing some structure. From these rough notes you can begin the more careful task of preparing the course notes, which you will use in your delivery to the student. As a first step, arrange the material into an appropriate sequence and into topics, as suits your needs. Colleagues are happy to offer advice on this – usually conflicting, so be prepared to decide for yourself.

Course notes

Your tutor's notes are for your benefit, but the course notes must obviously be prepared with the students' interests in mind. So for the course notes you need to think as much about how you say it as what you say. What you produce for the students must be readily understandable within the context of their background and ability; it must not be too much for them to cope with and not so little as to compromise standards. New teachers have great difficulty with this stage – they invariably overload, anxious not to be seen to be undermining standards. It is a subject-specific area in which to seek a lot of guidance – from colleagues, books, past examination papers if available and your own course material from your student days.

Two major guiding principles in preparing the course notes are:

i)   They must start at a point commensurate with the 'background' of the students. Nowadays the background is not always clear or reliable – you may have to determine it yourself.

ii) They must contain at least sufficient material to achieve the objectives of the course, at the required standard.

Writing style

Writing course notes is very different from, for example, writing a journal article. There is a lot of advice in the literature on how to write educational material, in a style suitable for various teaching methods and student backgrounds. At the risk of being hoisted by my own petard, I will list the twelve suggestions given by Rowntree (1966; see also Ellington and Race,1993) for educational writing:

– Write as you talk.
– Use the first person.
– Use contractions.
– Talk directly to the reader.
– Write about people, things and facts.
– Use active verbs and personal subjects.
– Use verbs rather than nouns and adjectives.
– Use short sentences.
– Use short paragraphs.
– Use rhetorical questions.
– Dramatize whenever possible.
– Use illustrations, examples, case studies.

Don't (or is it 'do not'?) regard these as prescriptions, but as ideas for developing your own style.

You can check out your writing for its educational effectiveness by a number of proprietary tests, some of a simple checklist type, and others of daunting mathematical sophistication. For most of us it is probably sufficient to reflect on any over-use of long words, phrases or sentences; unnecessary verbiage; pompous or slapdash style; inaccurate grammar, and so on. Objective tests for the effectiveness of educational writing include the *Cloze Test*, based on the ability of target readers to guess selectively deleted words; and the direct calculation of the reading age of the material provided by such numerical indicators as the *Modified Fog Index*. Such tests are, however, suspect at the higher education level, particularly in scientific and technical writing containing abbreviated text, equations and tables (Lewis, 1981; Ellington and Race, 1993).

How much material?

The course notes must take the student from an accessible starting point to cover the course objectives by the chosen teaching method. For each topic you have to decide on the amount of detail you intend to give the students and how much material you intend for their notes. This will depend on course content, your writing style and teaching method. With experience you will be able to establish your own rough and ready rules for the appropriate amount of material. For example, with standard chalk and talk, I find that about three A4 sides per lecture is about par for the course notes for a mathematics class. So for a 20 lecture course I expect to be looking at about 60 A4 sides of course notes. There will be problem sheets and worked examples in addition to this but so far as the main body of the course is concerned, that is about it. This works for me, but someone else may package the same intellectual content into 40 sides or 80 sides – horses for courses. Alternatively, try to estimate how much of a relevant text book you might expect the student to cope with in the available time – ask yourself how much *you* would reasonably cope with if the subject were new to you, remembering that you were probably a better than average student. In any event you will never get it right first time, and trial and error will be necessary in the first few deliveries of a course.

With an estimate of the amount of material you can cover in the time available, you now have to fit your treatment of the topics into this. Using handouts and directed reading you can exceed this but not by much. Within the course notes you have to fit the main ideas, results and argument/discussion comprising the course content. The overall sectioning and structure of the course should now suggest roughly how much space you can allot to each topic. At this stage you may be able to split the material into units suitable for individual lectures. You should certainly start to form an impression of the pace of the material throughout the course. Don't forget that for each topic you will need to introduce the essential results, prove them if necessary, illustrate and discuss them, apply them (all very subject-specific). All this must be fitted into your course notes and will give some idea of the depth of treatment you can afford. If you feel this leaves you short in some crucial topic then be careful how you resolve this. You can only justify a limited increase in one topic before you start chipping away at the others. You may have to settle for a more superficial approach to some other less essential topic. If every topic requires more time then either the course must be extended, or something must go.

Open learning courseware

If you are using open learning methods, placing more onus on the student to learn the material independently of you, then your courseware must obviously be adequate for the purpose. This is a question of degree. In principle, any students admitted to university should be capable of learning a subject for themselves from a good textbook, with lots of graded examples (although school textbooks are now far more user-friendly than those students are likely to find on university library shelves). So why not simply recommend a good textbook, tell them the date of the examination and have nothing more to do with them, apart from the occasional consultation? That is not, of course, why they pay money to come to university. Apart from all the other (more interesting) things which attract them to university, they come to learn more quickly, efficiently and effectively, as part of a coherent, structured programme. If you are going to require them to teach themselves to some extent, then you must provide the best supportive facilities. This takes time and commitment. Open learning is not simply about cutting down on your lectures and giving the students work to do. The same may be said about active learning in lectures – the activities require thought and careful preparation.

Self learning materials are available off-the-peg in some subjects, but you are unlikely to find something specifically customized to your needs. In future years, I can envisage the time when there will be a nationally available collection of such teaching materials for the core fundamental topics – such as may, for example, be covered in a typical first-year mathematics class in an engineering degree. But at present you will probably have to prepare your own material, or adapt someone else's.

Open learning courseware, to be fully effective, needs to have the following key features (Race, 1989). It needs to be:

INTERACTION CENTRED, involving the students in activities from which they learn.

MOTIVATING, interesting and involving the students, rather than taking their motivation for granted.

CONFIDENCE ENHANCING, providing regular positive feedback, increasing the students' self esteem and self reliance.

RELEVANT, making the students think it is purpose-built for their needs.

FLEXIBLY STRUCTURED, allowing the students to map their own structure on to the material as they learn, increasing their feeling of ownership.

INTERACTIVE, including lots of self-assessment questions with comprehensive responses, giving reasons for incorrect answers, as well as the correct answers, and detecting incorrect assumptions at the earliest possible opportunity.

CAREFULLY FLAGGED, with objectives clearly stated, accompanied by directions for achieving those objectives.

USER FRIENDLY, having a friendly conversational style – 'you and I' instead of third person passive.

PARTLY BLANK, containing 'white space' for students to enter their own contributions, solutions to exercises, additional notes, again increasing the feeling of ownership.

ACTIVELY VISUAL, with such things as diagrams and graphs forming the basis of activity such as amendments, interpretation, labelling axes.

EASILY DIGESTIBLE, presented in small easily managed pieces, each self-contained, to accommodate the limited concentration span of most people.

ADVISORY, advising students on the skills and study methods they will need; summarizing and reviewing material they need to understand and objectives they have to achieve; giving a study timetable against which to measure progress.

CONTINUALLY MONITORING performance, apprising students of their progress.

SUPPORTED by appropriate teacher and tutorial support and possibly by computer-aided learning, or distance learning facilities.

The previous comments should give you an idea of the considerable extra effort involved in producing open learning courseware as against conventional lecture notes or even a textbook. The extra time required in preparation (estimates range from 10 to 100 hours preparation per hour of learning – see Ellington and Race, 1993) must be set against any savings in staff contact time, although of course the bulk of the preparation is only required in the first year of presentation.

Concise, efficient and effective communication

Make the course notes as concise, efficient and as effective as possible, within the context of the subject (in mathematics, minimize the prose – hardly sound advice in English literature!). Look for the quickest means of getting your message across, drawing shamelessly on the experience of your colleagues at every opportunity. Use diagrams, flowcharts, etc. to provide and illustrate structure in addition to, or in place of, prose. Use mnemonics and other aids to memory – medical teaching would be impossible without them.

Explanation is not easy

The course notes should be clear and unambiguous – to the students, not just to you. If you have little experience of explaining complicated ideas to a novice, you will soon discover how difficult this is (Brown, 1978). First you have to establish a common language. Then you have to convey the desired information at a palatable rate. You have to make regular checks that the right message is being received by continually soliciting feedback. You will need to help the novice to utilize the information, to make deductions from it and apply it. Finally, you need to give the novice practice in the use of the new tools until the required proficiency is achieved. It is easy to teach the average person most things given plenty of time and lots of words – the trick is to teach the brighter person very complicated things as quickly as possible with the maximum economy of words. This is a skill that the good teacher will need to perfect – it is not easy. We can all remember a teacher who, with a few well chosen sentences, magically swept aside the mists of confusion left behind by predecessors in the treatment of some difficult topic. Things which help are: breaking the explanation into small palatable portions; keep asking questions; pause for thought; empathy.

In any subject there are a number of infamously difficult areas and some topics which you can cruise through. Try to spread the difficult topics throughout the course and prime the students for them in the course notes. Highlight these difficult areas, allow more time for them, pay special attention to their treatment, provide illustrative worked examples or additional discussion and make an extra effort to motivate the students. Pinpoint their relevance and importance in the course. Maybe you can approach a problem area from a number of different directions, or reinforce it by revisiting it at different points in the course.

Particularly essential items should be highlighted as such, by emphasizing them in the course objectives, for example. Extra practice should be provided in them. Remember that novices to a subject cannot easily discern for themselves what are the essential elements and unless otherwise directed will treat every sentence as equally important (or unimportant)! Conversely, if a particular topic is perhaps a little peripheral then it does not hurt to say so. However, students do not take kindly to being told a topic is non-examinable, having just sat through a lecture on it.

Not everything is simple or interesting

In preparing your course notes aim for simplicity and interest of explanation whenever you can, being as concise as possible, but do not struggle too hard to make everything rivetingly readable. In every subject there are hard, painfully boring topics which have to be accepted and waded through – just warn the students of these, commiserate and soldier on as enthusiastically as you can.

Say it three times

It is good practice for your course notes to fit the time honoured instructional format – *tell them what you are going to do; do it; tell them what you have done*. Thus the course might start with a brief, non-jargon (they have not learnt the jargon yet) overview of what the course is to achieve; then at the end you review the whole course, giving a checklist of what they should know – thus providing a basis for revision, in preparation for assessment. Individual lectures also benefit from such a three times format.

Depth versus breadth

You need to think about the depth and breadth of the subject matter of your course. The current trend in schools seems to be away from depth towards breadth and this is leading to a major problem in higher education today – the conflicting and irreconcilable demands of detailed proficient knowledge, against a rounded more portable appreciation of the subject. It affects you at both ends of the course – your students may not have the high level of background skill you would like and at the end of the course you will need to send them out appropriately equipped for the next stage in their education. If you decide to go for depth, then you have to cover less ground. You could perhaps get round this by giving additional 'optional' material as handouts, but if it is non-examinable, forget it – the students will. And if it is examinable, then you will be in danger of overloading. The same applies if you go for breadth and achieve the depth by additional handouts. You cannot buck it – the load on the student is measured by the area and for a fixed course duration must be roughly constant, so if you increase breadth you must decrease depth – end of story.

'Standards'

Try to avoid getting hung up on some absolute notion of 'standards' in your course. Take the example of the British system. Years ago, when the sixth-form curriculum was very tightly prescribed by the A-level syllabuses of just a handful of examination boards, with very close agreement between them and there was time to drill students in the core skills, then they *knew* what we wanted them to know and you could build on a fairly solid base. Then everyone knew what you could do in the first year and that set an absolute standard to aim for, with subsequent years following suit, culminating in a final degree of fairly widely agreed standards. In those times a statement like 'that topic is first-year material – it should not be in a second-year course' might mean something. No longer. I have seen good teaching staff founder by trying to cling to outdated notions of what a particular course *should* look like or *should* contain.

What students need to learn, not what you want to teach

Keep personal preferences in perspective. We all have our favourite topics and our pet hates in any subject and there is no harm in letting students get a glimpse of your individual tastes. But they are entitled to a fair, unbiased treatment of the full range of the subject. Indeed, the topics the teacher likes least are often the messy, boring ones – and it is precisely these which give the student the most trouble and therefore need the most careful treatment from you.

Beware of bias

No subject is so cut and dried that it is devoid of controversial issues and your courseware may contain contentious elements on which students receive alternative, or even conflicting, treatment from other teachers, textbooks or previous courses. Academics are often strong-minded individuals who sometimes find it irresistible to promote their own particular viewpoint. Try to avoid this by presenting alternatives objectively and showing the students that there are, indeed, controversial issues in your subject, on which they are entitled to their own opinion. This usually excites the interest and sympathy of the students, more so than a biased statement of your own perspective. Some teachers favour provoking students by dogmatic statement of their own views for the students to contest, but the debate is unequal and needs to be carefully handled.

Starting point of the course notes – the heterogeneous class

I've already referred to the difficult problem of where to start in the course notes and the need for good information about the student profile and background. The course notes must be intellectually accessible to the majority of students provided they put in a reasonable amount of work consistent with the standard of the course. (Make sense of that, if you can!) In levelling to a common starting point, one solution sometimes adopted is to excuse the better prepared students from some lectures/tutorials so that you can concentrate on the 'weaker' students. There is often a problem in deciding how to do this, however, because any given group of students may have a whole range of different weak spots despite similar formal qualifications. Even students with the highest grades can be seriously deficient in some crucial topics. Also, the object of a higher education is to stretch *all* participants to their limit, not to give some an easy ride because they have seen some material before. A tennis coach does not spend *less* time with his best players because they *are* the best. Put simply, every student is entitled to equal added value in their education.

In fact, the real situation is usually that each student, even 'the best', has weaknesses in some of the essential topics and the problem is to address these efficiently and effectively. One method is the use of short diagnostic tests in the key topics to identify the weak areas, which the student can then address with appropriate self-instructional material. If the better students progress rapidly through this, keep them occupied with more searching material. Note that the 'weak' areas may not simply be deficiencies in factual knowledge and skills but more serious problems, such as learning approaches used, inappropriate attitudes or lack of transferable skills. Corrective action in such cases can be very difficult and time consuming, but is even more essential.

It is particularly difficult to decide on the starting point of the course notes for interdisciplinary teaching where the class may have a very mixed background in your subject. While the students may formally satisfy the prerequisite qualifications for your course, the differing degree of commitment and motivation, and the differing attitudes and aspirations they bring from their different disciplines, must all be accommodated. Even worse, institutional imperatives for meeting required student numbers may lead to such a 'flexible' interpretation of entry qualifications that your students may be literally years apart in their background knowledge of your subject. You may then *have* to stream them – but how? By parent degree programme ? By grade of entry qualification, however unreliable?

In any class you teach, even one with a sound background, it is unwise to assume proficiency in all the prerequisite material for your course. For each new topic it is prudent to do a very quick thumb-nail sketch of the background material they will need for it, even if they have recently covered that material. Indeed this serves to ensure continuity of subject matter.

Organization and structure of the course notes

From the starting point and the course objectives you will have an idea of the sorts of topics you need to cover in your course. How these are presented in the overall structure of the course notes is important. Good logical structure assists the students in assimilating and memorizing the subject matter. Means of achieving this have been mentioned in Chapter Two (page 16) which apply equally well to the course notes.

Allocating subject matter to contact periods

Having prepared your course notes, so that you know what it is you wish to transmit to the students, you will need to divide them into suitable portions for individual lectures or as appropriate to your choice of teaching/learning activity. Preferably, do this in such a way that each lecture is devoted to complete topics, so that it is essentially self-contained. Try to avoid finishing lectures in mid-sentence! In allocating course notes in this way, remember that you may want a week or two at the end of the course for revision. Also, you may need to set some periods aside for tests. There is also the curse of bank holidays, fire practice and other sundry days out of the teaching calendar.

It is helpful if you can specify your lecture topics for each week in advance of the course and tell the students. Don't do this at the expense of flexibility, however. Sometimes you may be requested to present certain topics at a specific time. If you accede to too many such requests you may find yourself trying to give the whole course in the first week, so be sensible. Do what you can to assist colleagues but accept that in some cases, students will simply have to wait for a particular topic. Of course, if you issue a complete teaching package at the start of the course, then students can read ahead if they wish.

Ideally, the course notes for each lecture should have the usual 'three times' pattern – tell, do, remind – and should contain an element of motivation for the topics of that lecture. Warn the students of boring or tough topics coming up. Indicate the relative difficulty and importance of the different topics/items, being very specific about what material is examinable.

Delivery material and student's notes

Teaching material and equipment for delivery

With the course notes prepared and an idea of the activity and supplementary material required, with a comprehensive problem bank, then you can start to prepare delivery material and the material which will be issued to the students. This may include copies of the syllabus, OHP transparencies, tutorial material, problem sheets, book and reading lists, coursework, specific handout material (eg formulae sheets, complicated diagrams, tables, revision sheets, etc), tests, examination papers and other items, as required. An excellent text here is *Producing Teaching Materials* (Ellington and Race, 1993). They will even tell you how to hold the chalk! This section can only provide the briefest summary of the methods available.

Preparation for chalk and talk

'Chalk and talk' requires the least preparation. You may need to practise transcription of the notes on to the black (white) board to get the pace and presentation right. You should be sufficiently familiar with the notes to avoid *constant* reference to them, although there is no harm in regularly consulting them, so have them before you. Five to ten minutes spent reading the notes prior to the lecture are very helpful, no matter how familiar you are with the subject matter. If you are really on top of the subject, then you may find it sufficient to prepare a set of cue-cards containing reminders of the essential points.

Preparing OHP

If you are using an overhead projector (OHP) you need extra time to prepare the transparencies. You may be tempted to write these as you go along in the first presentation of the lecture, but this is not advisable. Writing tidy, well structured, notes on OHP transparencies from scratch is actually quite difficult. Do not overcrowd a transparency, avoid the edges (working on a cardboard template of the OHP platen helps here), use a sharp pen with a clearly visible colour (red, orange and yellow are all poor) and remember the students may not have different coloured pens. The most easily read writing or printing style seems to be lower-case print. Keep diagrams simple. Nowadays you can print OHP transparencies direct from a word processor.

Some people recommend that letters written on OHP transparencies should be at least 5mm. This is good advice if the intention is that the students copy everything from the OHP, but is not so essential if the OHP is being used as a visual aid to complement other material. The overriding imperative is that *all* students can see clearly *everything* that you *intend* them to see, and the only way to ensure this is to try your transparencies out in the classroom.

If you supplement the transparencies with chalk and talk, indicate clearly the relationship between the two. For example, at some point in the notes you may do a worked example on the board – show where this needs to slot into the notes on the transparency.

Preparing handouts

Allow time for preparation of any handouts, giving thought to what these comprise and when they are to be issued. You may issue just an occasional handout containing material difficult to display on the board or transparency – a complicated diagram or a lengthy table. Indicate how such things fit into the notes. If you copy these from a book or journal, check out the copyright laws. On the other hand your handouts may simply be the full set of course notes or fully supportive open learning material.

As for boards and transparencies, handouts should be tidy, not over-crowded, have key results highlighted, be arranged in sections and preferably typed. Imaginative use can be made of different coloured papers – white for notes, yellow for problem sheets, etc. Investigate what reprographic, printing and visual aid facilities are available in your institution. You invariably find that they can produce impressive results that you would never dream of.

Preparing other media

'Chalk and talk', OHP and handouts probably cover what the vast majority of teachers use today. While there are many other types of presentations one could use (models, slides, film, audiotapes, videos, computer-mediated materials, etc – see Ellington and Race, 1993, for an exhaustive list), these usually require greater preparation time and more expensive dedicated equipment and accommodation. However, the basic principles are the same – tidy and well organized; audio/visual clarity; unambiguous; allow time for preparation; match to your educational objectives; do not use to cram more topics into your course, nor to make the teacher redundant.

Special mention should be made of computer-assisted learning (CAL) software, even though it is unlikely that you will be involved in preparing it from scratch as yet. You are more likely to be piloting (I didn't say 'pirating') or adapting some off-the-peg software produced elsewhere. Whatever the benefits of CAL, you should not underestimate the difficulties of even adapting materials, let alone producing them yourself. *Authoring languages* designed to simplify the process of producing CAL software are proliferating at a healthy pace, and in future years it may be quite easy for you to write your own, but at the moment it is probably more cost effective to contract such production out – and then it only becomes viable if the class sizes are very large, in which case your accommodation and equipment costs rise. I suspect that unless their institution is making a determined, well-resourced push in some aspect of CAL, then most teachers will prefer to wait and see on this front. For an introduction to CAL see Barker and Yeates (1985), and for a brief overview and literature list on preparing CAL material see Ellington and Race (1993). For a more comprehensive treatment of the possibilities of all aspects of educational technology in higher education see Laurillard (1993).

Student activity and supplementary material

Student activity material

Just as important as the course notes is the material required to engage students in gainful learning activity. For many subjects this may consist of a series of problem sheets for the student to work through, but there are many other possibilities, for example laboratory work, for which they will need instructions. This activity material is essential in enabling the student to consolidate knowledge and develop skills. It also gives some idea of the relative importance of topics covered, the standards expected, the 'tricks of the trade' and, of course, the progress of the students. You will also need material for assessment. This is dealt with in Chapter Five.

Problem bank

I find it useful to construct a comprehensive problem bank as I work through the preparation of the course notes, generating many questions in each topic, of all standards of difficulty. This helps you to explore all the intricacies of the subject, identify areas of potential difficulty for the students and will also provide a useful resource for constructing problem sheets or worksheets, coursework, tests and examination papers. Problems may be routine, providing repetitive practice in specific skills, reinforcing memory, hammering home key points and so on. Others may be more searching, forcing the student to link ideas together, think laterally and examine topics more deeply. You may also need to prepare specimen solutions to some problems – for example, to self-assessment questions in open learning materials or to examination questions for external examiners. You may find it useful to build up a stock of these too.

Construction of problem sheets

With a good problem bank the preparation of problem sheets or worksheets in general should be a routine matter, but give careful thought to the structure of such things as problem sheets. This is where the real learning is done by the student. There is no other way to get your points across, or develop the skills you desire in your students, than by providing repeated exercise and practice in these. Problem sheets should broadly follow the course notes; the numbers of questions on each item should be commensurate with its importance in the course; a lot of short, routine questions is more effective for developing confidence than a few, longer, tough ones; insert some questions exercising previous material to reinforce it; include examination-standard questions; sprinkle a few real nasties to keep the best students on their toes. You can also use problem sheets to develop material additional to the notes, which you think is of interest – but it is only fair to indicate whether or not this is examinable. More general types of worksheets may be designed on similar lines (Ellington and Race, 1993).

Supplementary material

The course notes and activity material provide the core material for the course. In addition to these you have also to prepare the supplementary material you intend to provide. The latter will include things like the syllabus, book lists, directed reading and administrative information.

Book lists and directed reading need careful thought. As you construct your course notes you will probably get a good idea of suitable text books to recommend to the students. Inform the library and local bookshops of your requirements. If you must recommend a book for purchase, try to find a cheap paperback edition. Peripheral background reading will generally be ignored if it is not examinable. Directed reading is probably more effective if used in conjunction with an assessment procedure such as coursework.

It is helpful if your supplementary material also includes administrative information such as timetable, personal tutoring arrangements and your office times of availability. Give a precise written statement of the assessment procedure for your course (proportion of marks for coursework, for example) and ensure that all students are fully informed about this. This includes things like the rubric (see page 91) and the facilities such as computers, programmable calculators or sets of standard tables which may be used in the exam.

Prepare supplementary material in good time. A book list before the course starts; a specimen examination paper in the second half of the course, etc. Reference materials such as formulae sheets or statistical tables are best issued early on, so that students can become familiar with them. Pay regard to general points such as availability of literature or the relation of reading lists to the notes.

The students will appreciate a summary/revision sheet, which summarises the key definitions, concepts and results of the course. This serves as an expanded syllabus and is easily distilled from your course notes. In fact, it is a useful learning exercise for the students to prepare their own revision sheet.

Helping your students to learn

Particularly for first-year students, you might consider recommending some general reading on study methods and any other aspects of university life. After all, the better prepared the students, the better they will perform on your course. It also demonstrates your concern for their interests. Also, if you require them to use a non-standard study technique such as computer-assisted learning, then you may need to provide some training in this. There are many books on study methods suitable for students (it is invidious to make a choice, but Casey, 1985; Maddox, 1988; Meredeen, 1988; Shepherd, 1987 and Smith, 1990 spring to mind). Books written for teachers, to help them help their students to study effectively, include Devine (1987), Entwistle and Ramsden (1983), Gibbs (1981), Habeshaw et al. (1987), Maxwell (1980) and Raahem et al. (1991). I mention a large number of such books because this is a very important area - helping your students to learn. Indeed you might say it is *the* main purpose of teaching.

Evaluation material

You may also need to prepare material to be used in evaluating the course, or your teaching. This may include student questionnaires, checklists for self-evaluation and classroom observation and so on. Evaluation of teaching is discussed in Chapter Six.

Chapter Four

The Teaching/Learning Activity

The human side of teaching

A confident and positive approach

Teaching is difficult and stressful. You worry about the performance of the students; the maintenance of standards; whether you are getting your message across; if there is enough time for the material; simply standing up in the classroom and trying to command some attention. 'Is this really a bad class, or is it me?' 'Why was their last coursework so bad?' 'Their last test results were too good, have I pitched the standard too low?' Experienced teachers know that these questions never go away – and can find a lot more. So, if you are nervous about teaching, join the club! If not, you should ask yourself what pitfalls you have failed to notice, yet. This chapter is as much about coping with the stresses of teaching as with the technical aspects of specific teaching methods.

It helps if you have confidence that your job of teaching is worthwhile and something you are proud of. Early teachers were held in high esteem but since the days of Shaw's fatuous prejudice, 'those who can, do, those who can't, teach', teachers in general have been an easy target for sniping from those in the 'real' world. You might argue, like Eble (1976), that teaching *is* doing. I wouldn't waste the time. I prefer to comfort myself with the words of Gould (1991), '. . . the most noble word of all human speech, my teacher'. I am confident that my teaching is as worthy an activity as the next. If you can adopt this positive attitude too, are aware of the difficulties in teaching and the stress you have to cope with and have confidence in what you are doing, then you can concentrate more easily on the technicalities of the job.

Be prepared

By the time you walk into the classroom your preparation should be watertight. You should be completely on top of your material and have a clear idea of what you are going to do for the duration of the lecture, even if you intend to be flexible about what you do. Good preparation gives you confidence and impresses the students. Thoroughness and professionalism are respected – even by students.

The human side

With courseware and delivery materials thoroughly prepared, you can concentrate on the problems of *communication, human relationships* and *motivation* involved in producing an effective learning environment. In each of these crucial areas there are specific technical skills which can be developed, to facilitate the teaching/learning activity – skills of presentation, structuring the student activity and relating the subject to the interests of the students. But just as important, far more difficult and often glossed over altogether by writers on teaching, are the human facets of these activities. These are often the things which cause teachers, particularly inexperienced ones, the most trouble. Frequently a teacher is not asking, 'How do I prepare OHP transparencies?', but 'What do I do about the chattering in class ?' or 'How do I handle aggressive complaints about my coursework marking?' Teaching is, above all, an intensely human and interactive activity – if it is not, then you are not doing it properly. So I am going to devote some time to this 'human side' of teaching and try to address some common difficulties.

Communication

By 'communication' I mean more than just talking clearly and audibly *to* students. You will know what I mean if you think about a relative, friend, colleague, whom you 'have difficulty communicating with', even though you can talk to them. You 'just cannot get across' or 'we are not on the same wavelength'. But in effective teaching this is precisely what you must try to do – you must have empathy with your students. This requires objectivity and detachment from your personal feelings for the individual – qualities more usually associated with the counsellor, or the clergy. But if you can develop and maintain empathy with your students it is one of the most powerful tools for communication you have – it is something which the best teachers adopt naturally. How you do it is a matter for you. It helps to regard students kindly, give the benefit of the doubt, respect them, remember your own difficulties as a student, take students seriously without treating them seriously. Never attribute generalized characteristics to them to excuse deficiencies in your own teaching – 'No wonder 60 per cent of them failed the examination, they just don't work like they used to' reveals more about the teacher than the students.

Human relationships

As you are engaged in persuading bright, individualistic human beings to undertake difficult and possibly boring tasks and to perform at a high and stressful level, you are involved in human relationships at their most volatile. This is where inexperience shows (at both ends of the profession – new teachers dealing with well-known situations, experienced teachers dealing with novel situations) and is the most difficult to advise upon. The good news is that most of the skills required here are common to everyday life and you have probably been practising them since you were born. The bad news is that you may be poor at them – particularly in front of a class of perceptive, articulate, critical and witheringly forthright students. For those of you who have amused yourself at the expense of some hapless educator in the past, nemesis awaits. The general rules are: have confidence (but not too much) in yourself and your position; extend courtesy, consideration and respect to the students; give them their money's worth; be reliable; be firm and fair – and have a few effective sanctions tucked up your sleeve when all else fails. To be truthful, I cannot think of many such sanctions – expulsion from the class, report to head of department, etc, but these are absolutely the last resort.

Motivation

Motivation? I wish I knew. Your preparation is good; you are really getting your message across and your students think you are wonderful. However, all the majority of them want is a good class of degree, so that they can command a salary somewhat higher than yours. Perhaps the best way to motivate students is to develop a good rapport with the class, to fire them with your enthusiasm and persuade them of the interest and importance of your subject – not easy. It is sometimes possible to improve the motivation of students by choosing examples relevant to their interests, taking advantage of any topical issues or events involving your subject, and relating your material to the rest of their programme. Repeated reference to the examination helps too.

Personality and disposition

You will inevitably be part of any communication problem and you might give some thought to how you can redress your contribution. Obvious technical characteristics, such as quiet voice or untidy writing, can be dealt with if you are alert to them and prepared to spend a little time training yourself. More difficult are questions of your personality and attitude. I have seen little evidence that human beings are capable of doing much about this. The diverted nervous energy required to significantly modify your behaviour in a teaching situation could probably be better utilized in other ways. The thing you can do, however, is to alert the students to any personal quirks or attitudes which you feel may affect your teaching – if you know you are naturally impatient, tell them so. They will appreciate your honesty and be less inclined to blame themselves for incidents which may, in fact, be your fault. Examples of such personal difficulties are intolerance to students' queries; waffling aimlessly around a point; 'talking down' to students, and inappropriate *bonhomie*. Related to this is the need to be alert to your personal feelings and the ability to control them in a classroom situation. In a sense you should put yourself in the role of an objective, honest broker. No teaching activity, no assessment or expectations of a student should be unduly influenced by your personal feelings for that student.

Changing mood of the students

Make allowance for students' feelings, fears, aspirations and expectations in the classroom, particularly in the first few classes — as always, first impressions are lasting (Lowman, 1984). Unless your reputation has preceded you, most students will look forward to the first classes optimistically and will be prepared to give you the benefit of the doubt. Even if you do measure up in initial meetings, morale will still decline after the first few weeks, as the amount of work gathers pace. However, things usually pick up again quite quickly – and you can facilitate this – as students get into a steady comforting routine of work and begin to get some positive feedback. Things then go quiet for a while until examinations start to loom and the tension rises. They find it easier to locate your room at odd hours now and are unusually attentive for examination hints – many students put far more ingenuity into trying to predict the examination than they do in actually sitting it.

Student types

It is only human to categorize our fellows into personality types and it is inevitable that this should extend to our students. Some authors (Mann *et al*, 1970) have suggested various student types of this sort, the recognition of which is supposed to assist in our teaching. Personally I don't find this helpful. It is particularly objectionable when it is done in a derogatory manner to excuse lack of commitment to them. Students, as much as anyone else, need to be treated as individuals, not as subsets of the crowd.

One student type we are all pleased to see and happy to recognize is the 'gifted student'. In fact, the really gifted student is sometimes quite a nuisance and can go undetected as a result, their talent masked under a troublesome exterior. Watch out for these and put some effort into cultivating them. One of the great joys of teaching is watching the occasional surly, uncooperative, recalcitrant student transform into a gifted, successful achiever – they are the students you remember years afterwards.

Look out for students with special difficulties. There are many examples – physical, emotional or psychological handicaps; mature students with family commitments; self-financing; racial, sexual, religious minorities; committed elsewhere (sport, union, guild, etc). You cannot lower standards for such people, but it is helpful if you can demonstrate practical efforts to minimize their difficulties so far as your course is concerned (Lowman, 1984).

Some ideas from the theory of learning

The role of theory in teaching and learning

The title of this book should not be taken as a lack of interest or regard on my part for theoretical contributions to teaching and learning. Rather it is a reflection of the sad fact that because so few of us receive any sort of training in teaching, it *is* inevitably a practical subject for most of us. With the best will in the world few practising university teachers can afford the time to do more than scratch the surface of the vast literature produced by educationalists, let alone sort the wheat from the chaff. There is, however, a great deal of good theory about, of real practical use, and I would certainly encourage reading in this area.

One can distinguish between empirical studies, such as experiments or surveys, which gather evidence to test some hypothesis concerning teaching or learning; and conclusions based on accepted theories in sociology, psychology or even neurobiology. An example of the former is the study of the relative merits of note-taking versus the use of handouts, described in Bligh *et al.* (1981); or the debunking of the myth that students change their views of teachers significantly over time, described in Lowman (1984). Such results make interesting reading at the least, and can provide valuable insight and practical guidance at best. However, be wary of conclusions reached, since for every claim you are likely to find an equally convincing counterclaim. An example of the use of sociological theory is provided by Lowman's construction of a two-dimensional model for effective university teaching based on Bales's concepts of task and maintenance functions of group leadership (Lowman, 1984; Bales, 1950). Whatever your view of the outcome of such applications of theory, they do provide a framework for discussion and, more important, they get you thinking about your own teaching. However, as I have mentioned elsewhere, no such theories merit slavish adoption. Bligh *et al.* (1981) is a good objective introduction to the craft of weaving together theory and sound practical teaching experience.

Some writers on teaching advocate that you 'experiment' with your teaching methods – try out new ideas. While not discouraging this, I have seen (and perpetrated) enough disastrous experiments in teaching to urge caution. Students are not guinea pigs. Most subjects have a fairly standard and widely accepted 'most appropriate' teaching method and you should depart markedly from this only after much thought, consultation, preparation and justification of your actions, and certainly not on the basis of some vague theoretical argument, or to inflate the shares of some educational software company. 'New' methods and new technology are regularly arriving on the market, but much of it compares unfavourably with the accumulated wisdom of centuries of instruction and learning. The rapidly expanding possibilities for CAL probably provide the next great opportunity for experimentation with teaching methods, and on using such possibilities I cannot do better than quote Newble and Cannon's (1991) caution: 'We must not be seduced by the novelty nor must we let the opportunities they present pass us by.'

If you invest some time in reading some elementary theory of learning, then that may help you to gain some insight into the kind of learning difficulties students experience (and do not assume the best students are devoid of learning difficulties). Also, the students' learning processes may influence your teaching and, in turn, you may be able to influence learning processes to the good. But keep things in perspective – you are unlikely to turn yourself into an expert on the subject and there is no guarantee that it would improve your teaching if you did. For your first forays into the theory of learning you may prefer to choose books which are closer to the practical end of the spectrum. Good starters include Beard and Hartley (1984), Entwistle and Ramsden (1983), Ramsden (1988), Brown and Atkins (1988) all firmly rooted in practical utility. Also, Newble and Cannon (1991) provide, in their final chapter, a delightful cameo on helping students to learn.

Approaches to learning

Everyone has a different and ever-evolving approach to learning influenced by our own personality and *learning style*, the teaching methods used and other environmental factors. Teaching methods and environment tend to be the major determining factors, as most people can adapt their learning style. The approach used leads to a particular *learning process* by which the desired *learning outcome* is achieved.

The three broad approaches to learning in most common use are (Newble and Cannon, 1991):

- The *surface approach*, primarily motivated by desire to complete the course and relying on memorizing factual information, with a rote learning process, resulting in an outcome of mainly superficial understanding.
- The *deep approach*, primarily motivated by an interest in the subject, aiming for an outcome of thorough understanding of the material. This is usually achieved by one of three broad learning processes. The *operation learner* relies on logical, sequential approach, proceeding cautiously from one idea to the next. The *comprehension learner* aims directly for broad outlines of ideas, using analogies and fitting the knowledge into their own personal world view. The *versatile learner* combines both operation and comprehension processes, aiming for deep understanding buttressed by a sound factual knowledge.
- The *strategic approach* is mainly motivated by the need to compete and better others, achieving high marks and using any process conducive to this, usually resulting in a variable level of understanding depending on the requirements of the assessment procedure. These students 'play the system'.

Is there a best approach to learning?

Beware of hasty value-judgements on the above approaches. Each may be equally valid and appropriate in a particular context. During the Second World War fighter pilots, in critically short supply, *had* to use a strictly surface approach to learning, and who would question their effectiveness? On the other hand, if a student's prime objective of his three years at university is to get a first class degree, full stop, then what is wrong if the strategic learning approach accomplishes this in the quickest way? He has done the job. Further, one path to the deep approach is to first adopt a surface or strategic approach to get an overview and provide motivation and then to dig deeper. That is my preferred strategy. I have great affection for the words of the nurse of the blind, deaf and dumb Helen Keller – dismissed by everyone as unteachable – '*Imitate* first, *understand* later!'

Encouraging the deep approach

While we would all like to think we both encourage and realise the deep approach in our students, the reality is that we probably fail in most respects in this. Some people blame our teaching methods or assessment procedures, which they claim inhibit the use of the deep approach. Often it is simpler than this – we just overload them with too much material so that nothing gets treated in depth and their understanding is inevitably superficial. An example from my own discipline, mathematics, illustrates this. The amount of time available for teaching mathematics to engineers has been progressively reduced over the last decade or so, as other subjects such as computing and business studies have been introduced into the curriculum. At the same time, students are entering university with a weaker foundation in mathematics. However, many engineering departments are loath to forego coverage of what they regard as essential mathematical techniques – indeed, they are ever keen to introduce more topics. As a result, more and more material is crammed into less and less time. A surface approach becomes inevitable and high achievers often emerge via a strategic, rather than a deep approach. A similar situation now exists in schools and I am sure that you will be able to identify like tendencies in your own disciplines. Quite simply, it is becoming increasingly difficult to maintain and promote a deep approach without radical revision of the curriculum.

Measures you can take to encourage the deep approach are (Newble and Cannon, 1991; see also Gibbs, 1992a):

- Include higher-level intellectual skills, such as problem-solving and critical analysis, in your course objectives.
- Build in teaching activities demanding deep understanding of the material, avoiding mere repetition of factual information.
- Increase the ratio of group-based and self-oriented learning to didactic teaching. Decrease the amount of factual material which needs to be memorized.

- Devote more contact time to helping students to understand basic principles. Encourage students to be self critical.
- Ensure that your assessment procedures contain a proper proportion of questions testing in-depth understanding. Testing little and often during the course by easily marked multiple-choice tests, for example, keeps the students in a permanently questioning and examining mode.
- Modify your teaching style to enhance and encourage the learning processes of the students.
- Encourage and train your students in effective study skills.
- Identify and address any factors such as social or psychological problems, or specific study skill problems which may be inhibiting your students' attainments of the deep approach.

Learning the hard way

One obstacle to encouraging the deep approach is the currently fashionable belief that learning must be 'fun'. Some learning is fun, and it obviously helps your teaching if you can make the students' learning activity enjoyable. But deluding students that their learning must always be easy or fun is not helpful. Most learning is in fact very hard work – a job to be done. The sooner one accepts that, the easier the job becomes. It is simply difficult trying to concentrate and think, even on subjects which interest you. Sometimes curiosity makes it easier, but in general, particularly for students studying for a degree, interest is lukewarm and then learning is hard. I teach mathematics to engineering students, so I am experienced at teaching people who have little interest in what they are learning – and I don't think they would describe the exercise as 'fun'. Instead, while trying to make the subject as relevant and as interesting as I can, I warn them that they are in for a hard time, and get them to buckle down to it. Like slogging up a steep Lakeland hillside in the mist and driving rain, there is nothing to be done but get your head down and do it, safe in the knowledge that the view will be worth it when you get to the top – you hope. Of course, some people find hard work fun.

Teaching methods

Lecturing by default

Your teaching method is one of the earliest things to decide upon. It goes hand in hand with your course objectives. To be frank, most people generally opt for the default option of the standard lecture supported by tutorials or laboratory classes – it is cheap, effective and most seem to operate that way. Planning and preparation are easy to organize around a set of lectures and tutorials, there is a wealth of experience in the method and the attendant workload is relatively easy to quantify.

The importance of the record of what you do

There are three major components to the teaching/learning activity – the material, such as notes and problem sheets, which is actually supplied to the student, your activity which accompanies and delivers this, and the activity in which you engage the students. In some respects, your activity is probably the least important of these components (no offence intended). Thus, for example, at the end of a lecture the really crucial thing is what the students take out of the door – if it is a good set of notes then that can cover a multitude of sins in the actual presentation of the lecture. But a riveting lecture, with a poor set of notes, is only as lasting as the short-term memory span. So, whatever *you* do, aim to send the student out with a sufficient record and adequate learning activities to achieve the objectives of the lesson. Then you can concentrate on making the actual teaching and learning activities as effective as possible.

Teaching methods

The most common teaching methods are listed in Chapter Two (page 26), summarized here for convenience and grouped in line with Figure 1 as lecture, group or independent activity.

LECTURE
   Formal lecture
   Active lecture
GROUP
   Tutorial
   Seminar
   Role play/games
   Laboratory classes
   Peer tutoring
INDEPENDENT
   Open or independent learning
   Private study
   Computer assisted learning

These titles are only intended to be rough categories – there does not seem to be consensus on the precise definition of the terms in a teaching context, in any case. Elton (in Hills and Gilbert, 1977; see also Percival and Ellington, 1988; Ellington and Race, 1993) introduced a similar classification, comprising mass instruction, group learning, and individualized instruction.

You do not know the meaning of the word 'controversial' until you become enmeshed in arguments over 'the best' teaching methods. 'Lecturing is old fashioned and of little educational value.' 'Open learning is the latest fad, expecting the students to teach themselves and is of little educational value.' These are the extremes of typical views of teaching methods. Most practising teachers, however, are sensible enough to realize that all teaching methods are valid in their context. We will use whatever methods best achieve our course objectives, within our resources. The formal lecture and tutorial seems to have been the pragmatic solution to this for most staff until recent times. Now, resources are declining to such an extent that even lecture contact time must be reduced, resulting in a move towards independent learning methods. In the following sections I consider the types of teaching methods available and the sorts of results they can achieve.

The teaching/learning environment comprises teacher and student activity in varying proportions and types. If the teacher delivers the course by lecturing for two hours a week, conveying information and instruction, while the students develop and exercise their skills in tutorials and in private study, then that is the conventional *formal lecturing* method. If the teacher prepares supportive teaching material, cuts down on formal lectures and facilitates students to learn for themselves, that might be called *open learning*. So teaching methods may be described in terms of the type of activity engaged in by the teacher and the students and the distribution of time between these. This also provides a crude accounting procedure for relative costs of different methods. The formal lecture/tutorial method is costly in terms of both staff and student contact time, whereas open learning methods require less contact time, but require more preparation time and production costs for the supportive material.

Lectures

The formal lecture method

In a *formal lecture* the teacher imparts information and instructions, interacting only infrequently with students, in the expectation that the material thereby conveyed will be adequately assimilated by further activity outside the classroom. The rest of this section and the next two are devoted mainly to this form of presentation. Small group teaching is discussed on page 73 and independent learning on page 77.

Criticism of the lecture

It is currently fashionable to criticize the formal lecture method as being inappropriate in the modern learning environment, when so many other methods are available, such as computer-assisted learning, active learning and open learning. Some authors claim that formal lecturing is only appropriate for certain objectives (conveying knowledge, facilitating comprehension), but not for others (applications, analysis and synthesis, evaluation and criticism). I believe that a properly designed and delivered lecture can achieve all of these objectives. Put bluntly, a lecture can achieve anything that can be done by talking to someone. Of course, it cannot perfect the students' skills – only their *activity* can do that and that is the purpose of the tutorials and their private work. Most teachers have never had any doubt about the function and limitations of lectures. Lectures are only there to lay the foundations, show the way, ease the passage, as the student works through the subject. To turn a lecture into an 'active learning' session, for example, may be seen as encroaching on this function.

Detractors of the lecture often forget that students share the responsibility for their education. You are entitled to expect them to take your lectures seriously and be conscientious about listening and note-taking and to make a real effort to combat the inevitable boredom. It is not entirely your responsibility to keep them awake beyond the nominal twenty minutes for which they can maintain concentration – you will do your best, but they must also contribute their own effort and attention. In fact, students themselves often prefer conventional chalk and talk because it slows you down and keeps them active, but not *too* active.

The purpose of the lecture

In a formal lecture you convey the subject matter essentially by telling the students what you want them to know, or by giving them instructions about some suitable learning activity. This will include factual information, concepts and instructions on how to develop the required skills and attitudes. Clearly, your job is not to read out a telephone directory, while the students note down the names and numbers (that is the caricature detractors of the lecture method often set up in order to knock down). Your job is to teach them how to use the directory for themselves. You have three major considerations in a lecture – what you intend to impart, how you present it and how the students receive it. Each requires preparation and thought. The students may be issued with a telephone directory – you do not need to read it out. You simply have to tell them the essential elements of the use of the directory – the necessary jargon, the structure of the information contained, the principles of accessing this information. Then you go through a few examples, preferably relevant to them (find the number of the student-loan adviser, for example) and finally, you set them a large number of graded problems to do in their own time. How do you present the key points ? Write them on the board, OHP, issue handouts? How do you maintain their interest and emphasize the crucial points? How do you ensure that they have an adequate record of the lecture and its purpose? All this needs to be considered in your preparation for the lecture and was dealt with in Chapter Three. What follows relates to the mechanics of the presentation of the lecture.

Chalk and talk

Probably the most common form of presentation. Dirty but effective. The modern version – white board and felt pen – is cleaner, but people have been known to get high on the fumes from the pens, and heaven knows what the long-term effects of these are. The main disadvantages of 'chalk and talk' are chalk-dust, labour of writing and waste of writing the same thing year after year. The students also see a lot of your back. Board work is, however, surprisingly helpful for developing rapport with the students. They warm to watching you work, rather than standing immobile at an OHP, and numerous opportunities for levity and interchange arise from your mistakes, illegible writing and battles with stuck boards.

Overhead projector

The transparencies (slides, foils, acetates or other terms) may be prepared beforehand and used repeatedly. They are very popular nowadays. Clean and easy to use. But remember that, as with boardwork, everything on the transparency must be visible, legible and tidily organized and students must have adequate time to take notes. Experience will reveal the optimum number of transparencies for a lecture. Resist the temptation to use your new-found leisure time, freed from the drudgery of the board, to rush through more material. Instead, while the students are writing down from the transparency, occupy yourself with the sort of erudite rambling around the subject so beloved of the academic – and totally ignored by the student. To vary things a bit, leave some things off the transparency (worked examples, some proofs) which you can fill in and discuss in the lecture – this keeps everyone busy.

Handouts

Issuing your notes as handouts is very useful in moderation. This frees everyone from excessive writing and allows discussion of the awkward topics. Requires considerable preparation time and resources. Handouts are a real temptation to overload students, which should be avoided. Also, don't use them to rush through the remaining syllabus near the end of the course, when you have miscalculated your pace in the earlier stages. If a stand-alone set of notes for the course is provided, then many students will use them as such and skip lectures ('can I have three sets for my friends?' becomes a common request). Probably best to use for outline notes, peripheral material and particularly complicated presentations (eg difficult diagrams, tables), still leaving plenty for you and the students to do.

There is evidence that students who are given handouts tend to have higher attainment than those who have to take notes (Beard and Hartley, 1984). This may simply be a reflection of the teacher's greater commitment and energy implicit in preparation of such material, but still it does seem to enhance the learning experience. It is also found that students like to annotate their handouts and that 'white space' or blank sections encourage them to take more notes. Leaving white space, or omitting subject matter, also lessens the likelihood that students will skip lectures because of the availability of handouts. Handouts for large classes can be costly – you may have to charge for them, and this will entail problems about how to collect the money.

Use of other teaching aids

What I lack the space for here is covered admirably and comprehensively in a number of specialist texts (Ellington and Race, 1993; Kemp, 1980), and a glance at these will alert you to the wide range of teaching aids available for your presentation. Also, Newble and Cannon (1991) is typically replete with practical tips for the preparation and use of teaching aids. Many of the basic principles for the use of such aids are shared with the more conventional methods mentioned above: ensure visibility and audibility, pre-test in the classroom, match to educational and subject objectives, look at it from the student's point of view, keep it simple, etc. Most important, there is little merit in using complicated teaching aids for the sake of it when a cheaper, more convenient method will do the job just as effectively, particularly in these days of financial stringency. On CAL in particular there is little to add to the comments made in Chapter Three (page 47), except to remind you that its use requires training for the students, just as much as for yourself.

Before the lecture

Finalize preparation

Your preparation should be complete to the point where the course notes can be easily delivered by whatever process you have chosen. If chalk and talk, read through your notes as a reminder, or prepare your cue cards. Have OHP transparencies, handouts or other audio-visual aids readily to hand and organized for easy access. You should know the subject matter of the lecture inside out. Also, have a clear idea of the *purpose* of the lecture – to motivate and inspire; to convey information; or to instil key concepts and attitudes. Finalize your plan for the lecture, including time and material for the component activities. Remember to allow time for activities such as distributing handouts and returning coursework.

Mental preparation

Remember that most people under-achieve in front of an audience – you cannot think as fast or as clearly as usual, self doubt arises more easily and confidence ebbs. This is the reason for thorough preparation and planning and the necessity for prompts and cues. But, in addition, the presence of an audience can also modify your behaviour and personality. You need to be alert to this, to monitor yourself and take corrective action when necessary. For example, a common reaction under pressure in a classroom is to bury your head in your notes and/or talk to the board. You need to realize when this is happening and have a ready-made antidote, such as deliberately establishing eye contact with one of the students. If you want an amusing and somewhat awesome account of mental and emotional preparation for the classroom have a look at McGee's personal memorandum in the absolutely unforgettable (has to be required reading for any university teacher) *Teaching the Mass Class* (McGee, 1991).

Classroom accommodation

Check out the classroom before the lecture, to ensure that all required facilities are functional, that there is plenty of chalk or felt pens and no one has stolen the board rubber (an advantage of arriving early is that if the rubber is missing, you can quickly 'acquire' one from the next classroom).

At the start of the course check that the room is comfortable for the students and yourself – large enough to comfortably accommodate the numbers, good acoustics, appropriate facilities, etc. Be wary of over-crowding – particularly in summer – because this can generate excessive heat, and external noise sometimes precludes opening windows. On the other hand, the acoustics are sometimes worse in a half empty room. Remember that a cold room is much worse for the students than for yourself – you can walk about to keep warm. Check that boards, screens and visual aids are visible from the students' seats. Also have a quick practice to determine the appropriate letter size on the board/screens and test a suitable voice level. If the room is inherently unsuitable ask for a change, ensuring that everyone is kept informed of this. If you need special facilities such as microphone, OHP, slide projector or audio-visual equipment, order these in good time – particularly if it implies the necessity of a room change.

Timing of the class

Pay regard to the time of the class; 9.00 Monday morning and 4.00 Friday afternoons are not popular, although they may be inevitable due to time-tabling constraints. Also, you had better provide sleeping berths for a class following three other lectures in a row. If you really do feel the time is inappropriate, ask the timetabling officer for a change and be prepared for a bit of horsetrading. It is a very important consideration, so do not be easily put off. If a problem does not emerge until the course/class commences then cope as best you can but sort it out at the first opportunity. Ask the student representative in the class to assist you with this, as student complaints often carry more weight than those of the staff. This also helps generate a sense of working together and, as a general rule, the more you can involve the class in responsible decision making, the better.

Know your students – and yourself

Remind yourself about the history of the students on your course. Which are their parent departments? What is their background? Who is responsible for their administrative, academic, pastoral supervision? For large, interdisciplinary classes you may need to liaise with a number of different departments, tutors and timetabling officers. Each may come with their own demands, requests, problems, and some of these may conflict, also some may come from staff more senior than yourself. This may worry you and you may be unsure of your position. Your position is that you are the person charged, by your department, with the conduct of that class – it is your responsibility. It is your considered judgement, after advice, which should prevail in such matters. If you defer to one person's requests against your better judgement, either through insecurity or simply to please, then this may have unanticipated knock-on effects for which *you* may well end up carrying the can. In general, be as helpful and accommodating as you can, but seek advice as soon as you feel uncomfortable about a situation.

It is helpful if you can meet at least some of the students before the course/lecture – maybe by arriving a few minutes early at the lecture – and have an informal chat. There is no need to behave out of character, feign interest or affect friendliness. If general social chat is difficult for you, engage in conversation about the course – have they seen any of the material before, what sort of preparation do they have, etc. This all helps to break down barriers between you and establishes a personal and co-operative atmosphere in the class, greatly enhancing the educational process even in large classes.

Presenting the lecture

Nerves

This is it, no more putting off the evil moment – you have to walk in, grit your teeth and go for it. If you psych yourself up sufficiently beforehand the experience will be less fraught than you expect, maybe even a bit of an anti-climax and gradually you may be able to relax. And I'm not talking about your very first lecture! I still feel nervous when meeting a class for the first time, and one of my most respected colleagues admitted, near retirement, that he still dreaded the first lectures of a new course. Beware of the cheap option of adopting a formal, autocratic, no-nonsense stance to quell (disguise) nervousness, intimidating the students into submission. It may work – until the first time you make a fool of yourself – but it doesn't help in developing rapport.

As with all forms of strenuous activity, the nervousness is essential for peak performance. It sharpens the senses, taps latent reserves of energy and concentrates the mind. The trick is to control it and make it work for you, rather than turning you into a bumbling idiot. This is best done by knowing the task you are there to do and throwing yourself into it professionally and single-mindedly. You have prepared yourself well, you know what you want to do in the lecture period; you have checked out the room and all the required facilities; you know a little about the students before you; you know your responsibilities and your professional status in relation to your students – now get on with it.

Timekeeping

Be punctual. This is common courtesy and you should expect it in your students. Sloppy timekeeping gives an impression of lack of interest in the activity and fuels students' righteous indignation. On the occasions when you are late, apologise and briefly explain the reason – not so much out of contrition, but out of courtesy and to promote personal rapport with the students. Make it clear to them that you expect similar courtesy. If you are unavoidably late try to contact someone to let the class know.

You may finish early, but never late – students may have engagements elsewhere and should be spared the embarrassment of having to rise and leave while you are still in full flow. You will have no trouble anticipating the end of the lecture – if you are in any danger of overrunning the students will commence noisily rustling their papers and ostentatiously opening their bags to put things away. Finishing early can allow time for a few questions, getting to know the students or to slip in some optional topics.

New teachers, particularly, have problems dealing with latecomers, being hesitant about exercising authority by insisting on punctual attendance – it is so much easier to just ignore people trickling in and noisily finding their place. But remember that as the person responsible for the class you should ensure that the majority of the *students*, not just yourself, are satisfied with the conduct of the lesson and my guess is that they would usually wish to start on time and minimize interruptions. Make sure everyone knows you expect the class to start on time and have a quiet word with persistent latecomers.

Performance and delivery

In the classroom you must be something of a performer, as well as an educator. From the outset you are delivering a message to the students and want them to assimilate as much as possible. This requires constant arousal of their interest and your presentation should be as arresting and stimulating as you can make it within the parameters of your own personality. Do not attempt to adopt a character that is alien to you – above all, be yourself. Because of the way you have been chosen for the job, that should be interesting and stimulating enough. But it is not easy to let yourself come through in front of an audience – you will have to work at it. You start from the moment you walk into the room. It is worthwhile to spend a minute or two just relaxing yourself and the class – let them settle down (tell them to if necessary), introduce yourself if the class is new, use a little small talk, a spontaneous joke if appropriate; or a few words about whether today's topic is difficult. Anything to break the ice, bridge the gap, get them looking your way. At first this may require some concentration and thought from you, but after a few classes you will find yourself doing it naturally.

Dr Fox

While you clearly need to engage the attention of the students, be careful that they do not focus on your personality, rather than the subject. The dangers of this are illustrated by the so-called *Dr Fox effect*. This was demonstrated in an experiment in which an actor, 'Dr Fox', delivered a lecture composed entirely of meaningless gibberish (don't we all?) to an experienced audience who were enthralled and went off perfectly satisfied with the informative and interesting lecture, fooled by the 'doctor's' animated and engaging delivery. In fact, many experienced teachers regularly get themselves out of trouble on losing their thread, by arm waving accompanying meaningless mutterings.

Agreeing the conduct of the lecture

At the beginning of a course come to an understanding with the class about how the lectures will be conducted. This can also include such things as the responsibilities of the students in getting work in on time and well presented. Come to terms on the *course* objectives, *your* objectives and *theirs*. How you reach this understanding is up to you, but it must be clear, unequivocal and reasonable. You and the students have a difficult task and need a conducive environment for it. You cannot talk to a class over a constant background of nattering and they cannot follow you if you write solidly on the board at a furious pace, without pause. Tell the students what behaviour you require of them, explaining that this is what you need to perform effectively. Agree to do your best for them, but if there is a problem – writing too small or voice level too low, for example – they should tell you immediately.

Opinions vary on this, but my feeling is that you should tolerate nothing which makes your teaching job more difficult and there should be no doubt that you are in charge of the proceedings. You should be in control of the class from the start. For example, there will inevitably be a bit of chatter here and there and to insist on permanent, total silence is counterproductive. However, the minute it becomes any sort of problem to you, attend to it. It is better to be firm and exert tighter control in the early stages of the course – easing up later if you wish – than to start off soft and have to regain control later. Actually, sad though it is, many students seem to *like* being told what to do.

Starting the lecture

Start with a brief outline of what you are going to do in the lecture (tell, do, remind). Put it into the overall context of the course; maybe you are continuing from the last lecture, starting a new topic, etc. It is probably best to get the various bits and pieces, like commenting on coursework performance, issuing material and administrative announcements, out of the way at the start to avoid a rush at the end. It often helps to start the lecture with a problem relevant to the students' interests and then base the lecture on addressing the problem – this provides immediate motivation.

Ensure satisfactory delivery

In your presentation of the material, consciously ensure that your delivery is satisfactory to all students in the class. Check that they can see everything they need to (with board and OHPs *you* are usually the main obstruction). Do not write/talk too fast. Leave material in view for sufficient time. Ensure your voice level is adequate and remember to talk to the students and not to the board. Use intonation, emphasis, changing voice levels, body language and the rest to enliven your delivery. Sound interested and enthusiastic (whatever you feel). Maintaining eye contact with the students stops you staring aimlessly into space or at the board – if you find this difficult, pretend by aiming your eyes at the students' notes. Eye contact also helps in monitoring the response of the students to your delivery.

If you get the opportunity, it is worthwhile having a little voice training early in your teaching career. This will help with projection of your voice, articulation and fluency. Some things you can correct yourself – try to cut down on the 'uhms' and 'aahs' and any persistent speech habits such as 'OK?', 'right', etc. I once walked into a lecture to find 'OK? right,' chalked all over the board, and a grinning class. It was the kindest way they could tell me – and it worked!

Your boardwork is important. Make sure everything on the board is clearly visible and legible for everyone in the classroom. Arrange your boardwork tidily, using a variety of means of highlighting section headings, important results, etc. – underlining, upper/lower case lettering, boxing. Keep reminding yourself that while you are aware of the context and relative importance of everything you write down, the *students are not* and the visual presentation should assist in conveying this information to them. You can write on the board faster than they can copy on paper, so allow time for your students to keep up with you. There is a great temptation when lecturing to scribble in any odd corner of the board – only do this with material the students do not need to record. Tell the students precisely what you want them to take down. Start and finish with a clean board. Wiping the board with vertical strokes reduces the dust cloud.

If you are using OHP and you are writing on the transparency, use a sheet of paper to avoid smudging; if already written and you wish to reveal point by point on the transparency, put the paper *under* the acetate. If you use a pointer on the transparency rather than the projection then you can remain facing the class, although brought-up-on-board teachers like myself find conversing with the screen irresistible.

What they see is what they get

Remember that what the students see is what they get – literally. Few students will note anything other than what you actually display to them and give them time to transcribe. They rarely note what you *say* unless they have time to listen to it – for example, if they have handouts supplied. The main purpose of what you say is to direct attention (by intonation and gesture) and to amplify the key points. Give careful attention to first use of new definitions and symbols. For example, when using Greek letters in scientific work, issue a handout showing the complete Greek alphabet, with the names of the letters. Avoid use of materials which may not be available to the students – for example, coloured chalk and pens.

Students' notes

The students' notes depend as much on their skills at note-taking as on your skills at delivering them. In their first year particularly, students may find note-taking difficult and may need some sort of training in this. Remember, as noted elsewhere, teaching/learning is a joint enterprise – your mode of delivery has to mesh with the students' ability to receive it. As an extreme example, if you intended to dictate everything at normal talking speed, then you would have to train them in shorthand. Again, your course notes can help a great deal here, by making the minimum demand on students' note-taking skills. Thus, always use the simplest form of expression; use diagrams, abbreviations, acronyms and so on, to best effect. Do not introduce too many new definitions, notations or ideas at once. Even if you give comprehensive handouts, structure them carefully and efficiently, since the students will still have to read them while you are lecturing, which is not easy.

Body language

Body movements and gestures can be very effective in communication in general and teaching in particular. The growth of acting schools is testimony to the fact that one can be trained in such skills, but again few of us have the time for this. Observe as many good speakers in action as you can and take any opportunity to attend relevant staff development courses, where you can often learn much with and from your colleagues. I prefer to teach standing up and facing the class, but you can stand on your head if you wish. Many teachers restrain themselves unnecessarily in a classroom, seeking gravitas in immobility and rigidity. Instead, use your energy; imagine you are talking to a close friend and let yourself go. Some frown on teachers who prowl about the room as they talk – personally, I cannot stand still, and provided I ensure that all students can hear me clearly at all times, I see no reason to forego the exercise. Helpful gestures include linking hand movements to inflection and speed of speech; highlighting areas of the board, or screen; itemizing points on the fingers of the hand; 'fist thumping' or hand waving to illustrate importance or irrelevance of a point. But again, all things in moderation.

The 20-minute boredom threshold – asking questions

To arouse and maintain interest it is often recommended that you change the format of the presentation about every 20 minutes – say by moving from ↖ formal lecture to a discussion period. This is based on the well-known learning curve for students during a lecture (Bligh, 1974) (see Figure 3). Learning declines after initial interest arousal, but may be revived by a suitable rest or interjection of novel activity. It may be even more advisable in the future to vary our lectures, as teaching methods in schools move towards a more interactive, experiential approach, with the result that students will no longer tolerate prolonged periods of formal lecturing. However, it may not always be practicable to vary your teaching format too much. Indeed, in many subjects, particularly with large classes, the formal lecture is probably the best approach. In that case you can break up the monotony by tossing leading questions to the students. Don't be despondent if the only response is a row of blank faces – students rarely share your enthusiasm for the subject. You may have to lean on them a little. The worst question you can ask is, 'Have you done …?', referring to something you know they are supposed to have done in a previous course. They will always deny any knowledge of this, depressing you and obliging you to

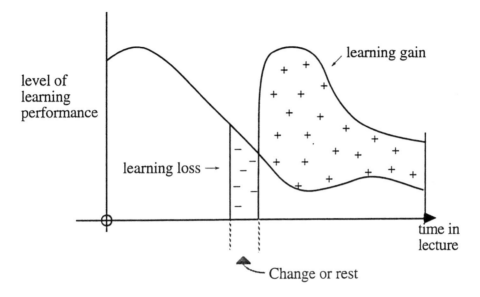

Figure 3 *Learning curve in a lecture*

quickly remind them. Some inexperienced teachers have been known to repeat whole courses by asking the wrong questions.

Monitoring progress

Frequent questions will also allow you to monitor the students' assimilation of the course content – you will *always* over-estimate their comprehension of the material and will have to probe, during class and in tutorials, to get reliable feedback. During the lecture be alert to the expressions and mannerisms of the students – with experience you will be able to read the state of play. If any student expresses obvious irritation (they like throwing their pens down and folding their arms in disgust) ask what you have done wrong. When you have got to know the students a little you will be able to pick out one or two whom you can rely on for feedback about how the lecture is going. Of course, if you find that the students are having genuine difficulty, either through lack of background, or inability to keep up, then you must address that, if not there and then, in a tutorial or private consultation. No matter how good your preparation, you will still have the unexpected problem to clear up and must be flexible enough to deal with this – ploughing on regardless is simply putting off the inevitable.

Brainstorming

For some material, particularly when basic ideas of a fairly concise type have to be hammered out of a vague surface view, a very powerful and enjoyable teaching method is provided by 'brainstorming'. This is nothing more than the free generation and association of ideas and suggestions within a group of people, which has always been a widely used and effective teaching tool – it is just that nobody bothered to give it a name (there are many examples where trainers and educationalists have built their reputations on simply naming well tried and familiar techniques).

In brainstorming, a problem is specified and everyone in the group throws in ideas, in a round-robin format for example, and these are recorded verbatim in a non-judgemental way. When time, energy or flip chart is exhausted, the group works through the list, rearranging appropriately, pruning obvious flops and any effective repetitions until a manageable, grouped, list of items and points is obtained, which then forms the basis for further discussions and developments. The method can be time-consuming and it may seem an inefficient way to arrive at the final conclusions, which are usually fairly simple – why didn't the teacher simply write them down to begin with and save everyone's time? This is not the point, however. The final conclusions will usually be more profound than they might appear and are worthy of in-depth consideration, with everyone actively thinking about their origins. I would not begrudge an hour of brainstorming which yielded up Newton's laws of motion, for example. The method serves other purposes too – it breaks down classroom reserve, builds links between teacher and students and encourages discussion after students have left the classroom. It is particularly effective for teaching project work, for example.

Mind your language

The way in which you talk to the students is important. Your tone should be sympathetic, helpful and explanatory. It is very easy to be short-tempered, intolerant or arrogant towards students, particularly when they try your patience, but you should avoid this. Respect your audience and try to give the benefit of the doubt. Never talk down to them, be sarcastic, condescending or patronizing. Personal remarks, sexist, racist, etc. are out. Bad language or other offensive behaviour are likewise taboo. Light-heartedness and humour in moderation is often quite useful, particularly if it reinforces a teaching point, but be sure you can carry it off.

Responding to questions

Respond to students' questions in class in a sympathetic and helpful way. Do not discomfort the student if it is a 'silly question' – or allow the class to. Respond with a quick answer if this is appropriate, but if you think it will take up too much time, deal with it after the lesson, unless it is a difficulty shared by many students and can be used to expand on a teaching point.

Learn to say 'I don't know' if you occasionally get stuck on a question, or a piece of work in the notes. Under classroom pressure it sometimes happens that you dry up or suffer a mental block. The tendency is to try and sort it out on the spot. You should only spend a few minutes on this and then say you will sort it out for the next lecture. You may find that minutes afterwards, with the pressure relieved, the solution occurs to you, but if not, no matter. There is no shame or harm in getting stuck on a point, even if you are the teacher. It is just a waste of everyone's time if you struggle on, digging yourself a deeper and deeper hole, with students hurling incoherent suggestions at you. Also, do not hide behind waffle – students spot it immediately. Just be open and frank – skip it and deal with it later. But make sure that you *do* resolve it for the next lecture – be reliable.

Talking too much

A quite common, unfortunate tendency of some of us is what might be called 'running off at the mouth'. This occurs in instances when a topic particularly interests us and on which we have strong, deep-felt views and knowledge. Propelled by admiration for our own erudition and determined not to deny students every last pearl of wisdom, we ramble on endlessly and hopelessly. Good preparation, discipline and time-keeping will avoid this embarrassment.

Tidy up after you

At the end of your lecture leave everything tidy and wipe the board clean, replace seats if they have been rearranged. Leave the room not as you would wish to find it but as your colleagues would wish to find it.

Evaluating and reviewing the lecture

After the lecture spend a little time assessing your performance and the learning outcomes of the session and considering how they might be improved. I am sure you will find yourself doing this automatically, but you may tend to focus on the good points (or on the bad) so try to be comprehensive and objective. You need to consider whether the notes conveyed the desired messages, whether the presentation was clear and to the point and whether the preparation time was sufficient. Also think about the reaction of the students. Do you think they were satisfied? Do you think they grasped key points you wanted to convey? Some people distribute questionnaires to the students after the lecture. Such evaluation of teaching is the subject of Chapter Six.

Active learning in lectures

Most of the comments above refer to the conventional mode of lecture, which basically amounts to an address by the teacher, taking a few questions from the students, or maybe introducing the odd distraction to relieve boredom. There are many ways one can vary the presentation and activity in the lecture to better achieve some objectives such as development of skills in applications, analysis, synthesis and evaluation (although often at the expense of content and efficiency). Essentially the object is to involve students in exchange and interaction, to encourage them to take charge of their own learning, and to facilitate their independence even in the relatively controlled environment of the lecture room. Means of doing this range from simple question and answer sessions to highly structured sessions, planned to the last minute, in which set tasks are performed at educationally appropriate points in the lecture. There are many advocates of active learning, in a number of countries, at the moment (CVCP/USDU,1992; Habeshaw, 1989; Gibbs and Jenkins, 1992; Race and Brown, 1993). It has to be said, however, that such initiatives will not excite the bulk of university teachers while they see their meagre resources diminishing further.

Question and answer (Socratic method)

Socrates liked to teach by establishing a dialogue with his student(s) – using questions and answers to crystallize a particular truth or concept. The main motivation behind the Socratic approach is to improve intellectual and oral skills and establish specific attitudes in the student – qualities which the formal lecture does not always encourage. The Socratic method is usually advocated for small-group teaching. For an example of Socratic dialogue in the lecture see Brown and Atkins (1988). Essentially, one guides the students to a desired objective by carefully chosen questions. It is at its best in a completely interactive environment, with a small number of students. The main difficulty with its use in large lectures is in getting participation from the audience. Often, after asking a few questions and receiving little response, the teacher gets fed up, answers them, and continues with the address. The method is then seen as perfunctory and fails in its purpose.

The Socratic method is regarded by some as time consuming in a large lecture, where it might be thought quicker to simply state the final conclusion. But again, as with brainstorming, knowledge of the conclusion is not the main educational objective of the method; it is training in the transferable skills provided by the dialogue and the deeper understanding thereby achieved. Many teachers who would like to teach in this way are deterred by the difficulties of establishing and maintaining dialogue in a large class and the pressures on 'covering the material'.

Getting a response

Make sure that the questions you ask the class are clear and relatively unambiguous, although they do need to be open, allowing a range of answers and promoting discussion. You may ask a question in a number of different ways. Give the students time to think, but make it clear you do intend that they think. Keep up the pressure and insist on getting an answer, but don't make individuals feel threatened – develop an atmosphere in which it is easy for any student to answer. Don't let a *single* student dominate the proceedings, but there is little harm if a group of, say, half a dozen students dotted around the lecture room always provide the response. The others will be thinking about it and will benefit from monitoring the dialogue – there will always be doers and observers in this world, with rather more of the latter.

It is often easier to get answers in a question-and-answer session if, at the start of the course, the class is divided into small groups with about five students each. You then direct the question at a particular group, after allowing some time for conferring, one of whose members is obliged to respond – the group decides on the spokesperson. Obviously the type of lecture accommodation and seating arrangement is relevant here and a large flat room with grouped tables is preferable but, failing this, it is not difficult to adapt to a tiered lecture theatre.

If your question-and-answer session is carefully designed, then you can prepare a handout with spaces available for written responses. People usually consider written responses more carefully. It gives them time to think, provides a record of the exercise, promotes discussion and interactive activity and affords some privacy. Then, in the absence of a timely response you can choose someone's answer sheet at random. All such activities require a little organization and thought, but once you get them started in the first year of delivery of the course, only fine tuning is required in subsequent years. If you collect and consult the handouts after the lecture, that will also provide you with feedback on how it went and encourage students to play the game.

The hyper-active lecture

One can, of course, introduce more varied activities than the simple question-and-answer approach into a lecture. I can leave it to your imagi-nation – the key thing is to fit the activity to the particular educational objective. For an example of a (hyper)-active lecture see that described by Alan Jenkins in Gibbs and Jenkins (1992). It contained six periods of teacher talk totalling 32 minutes, interspersed with several periods of student activity totalling 25 minutes. The method works well for quite large classes (over 100), but becomes difficult to organize in *very* large classes of over 400. (I bet!)

Jenkins advises introducing such active lectures gradually, allowing the best structure to develop from experience. Care should be taken to ensure that students understand the approach and the tasks used. He suggests that formal lecturing occurs only in short periods and each such mini-lecture is followed by an appropriate task, worked on in small groups. The tasks should also be varied and related to other major learning activities under-taken by the students. Remember that the method may require a range of print-based materials, needing preparation in advance of the activities.

Teaching in groups

The purpose of small-group teaching

By a *group* I mean, for teaching purposes, any set of students enabled to learn by their mutual interaction with or without the presence of the teacher. This includes the conventional tutorials and seminars, as well as workshops, self-help groups and peer tutoring. Usually the group is relatively small, depending on the activity – fewer than 10 in a seminar, up to about 30 in a tutorial. Books devoted to group teaching include Abercrombie (1974), Habeshaw *et al* (1989), Jacques (1991), and Lublin (1987). Good treatments may also be found in Bligh *et al*. (1981) and Newble and Cannon (1991).

The purpose of small-group teaching is to provide a stimulating environment for students, where the learning process is more by discovery, serving to alert students to gaps in their knowledge by exposure to the contributions of other students. The method also trains students in the communication skills required for constructive participation in team work and generating ideas by interaction. Small-group teaching by discussion concentrates on the *process* of learning, rather than on the *content*. Here, the teacher is a facilitator of the process and the content is obtained in the process of the discussion – it does not have to be provided by the teacher.

The precise aims of small-group teaching vary with each type of group. Thus, in the humanities one might aim to develop oral skills, the ability to cooperate, self-awareness and a sense of social identity, while at the same time providing the student with the opportunity for self-expression and giving staff feedback on how students respond to ideas. On the other hand, in a subject such as mathematics we would be using the interaction in small groups to convey knowledge and skills by example and immediate feedback, to promote understanding through discussion and the exchange of ideas.

Tutorial and seminar

The two most common types of small-group teaching are the *tutorial* in which students work on a prescribed topic, overseen by the teacher who guides and assists the students in their work, and the *seminar* where a student will present a paper and lead discussion on some topic – which the rest can pick to pieces. Be warned, however, that these terms may mean different things in different institutions.

Managing the small group

Effective small-group teaching requires good organization, with rules of order. It relies on participation to educate. The groups need to be chosen and managed carefully, to have the best chance of full involvement by all present – shutting up the excessively vocal, drawing out the quiet and timid. Some subjects lend themselves to small-group discussions better than others – the topics at issue need to be debatable, with many equally acceptable viewpoints, rather than the more cut and dried factual material. It is best if the group can run itself, the teacher acting simply as a resource or consultant. Ideally, students should do some preparation before the group meets – directed reading, some research, or preparing a paper.

Qualities required in a good group leader are: awareness of the mood of individuals, open-mindedness, responsiveness, the ability to draw people out, the skill to lead without interference and towards set objectives. Good powers of communication, interpretation and the ability to inspire respect and affection from the group are also advantages. The leader also needs to keep one eye on the clock.

To contribute effectively to group discussions the members should be encouraged to be non-dominating, considerate, confident in themselves, responsive to others, interested and involved in the proceedings in a cooperative way. Also, if they can challenge even the most universally accepted opinions, with sensitivity, playing devil's advocate if necessary, then that can be very stimulating.

Classroom accommodation for small groups

The general requirements for accommodation of small-group teaching are similar to those of small lectures – comfortable heating, lighting, acoustics, reasonable space. More care is needed in the seating arrangement – preferably in a circle or arc, with the tutor at one end or mobile. Particularly in the sciences and mathematics, everyone will need access to plenty of writing surfaces.

Participation and direction

There are two major problems in small-group discussions:

 i) getting full participation of all of the group,
ii) maintaining progress in the direction of the objectives of the course.

The teacher must be energetic and proactive in addressing these problems. Pull in students who keep quiet, and praise even infrequent contributions. Prevent any one person from going on too long or straying too far from the point. Facilitate communication between members of the group by clarifying vague contributions.

Exercise classes are not really groups

Many 'tutorials' are simply exercise classes with students working under supervision, on sets of problems. *Large* exercise classes are notoriously variable in their effectiveness. I can remember only a few energetic and highly committed teachers who could conduct them really well. Basically, the students rarely want to work in a controlled environment on set questions, often preferring to work in their own time. Attendance frequently drops rapidly. The teacher has to work hard, scurrying round the class, leaning over shoulders and badgering students in the nicest possible way, encouraging them to wrestle with their difficulties and to help each other out. The worst thing you can do is sit out front expecting the students to come to you – you have to circulate continually and generally be a pest.

Peer tutoring

If you are not able to stimulate students into activity in a group, then they may well be better off without you. *Peer tutoring* is the answer – leave them to themselves to get on with it (Entwistle *et al*, 1992). They may feel less inhibited without you there and may value the responsibility they have been given. They will, of course, just disappear if you do not set them a well-defined task, with an obligation to report progress to you.

Personal tutoring

The smallest group is one student. *Personal tutoring* is fast becoming an unaffordable luxury and yet it is obviously one of the most valuable and effective teaching methods. There are two common ways in which personal tutoring tends to occur – the formally timetabled meeting of fixed duration in which the student presents and discusses particular set work, and the informal spontaneous meeting when a student comes to see you about a particular difficulty he or she is encountering. I will call the latter *student consultation* – it can present wider teaching opportunities than formal personal tutoring and requires different skills on the part of the tutor, for maximum benefit.

Personal tutoring arrangements vary from institution to institution. In some cases the personal tutor may be a specific teacher allocated to a particular student and the tutor's remit is to cope with the student's personal problems as well as academic problems. Here, we are only concerned with the latter (although, of course, the former are very important too). The job of the personal tutor is not only to appraise the student's work, providing correction and reinforcement, but also to encourage, inspire and lead – ideally, the student should leave with as many (but different) questions as he/she brought. A warm and welcoming attitude will help to draw out the student. Also it is very easy for you to be forbidding and intimidating to the student without realizing it, so make a conscious effort to avoid this.

Student consultation

Impromptu student consultation – the knock on the door followed by a nervous student seeking help – is a very valuable teaching opportunity which should not be wasted. The student has a particular problem(s) and has taken the trouble to seek you out, so is especially receptive – and especially helpful, because he or she can give you an idea of the sticking points the students are having in general. And do not think of it as expensive private tuition. If you clear up the student's problem(s), he/she will invariably go back to classmates and enlighten them in turn. So, be welcoming, relax the student and deal with his/her difficulty, also drawing out any others there may be. If you have the time, you can turn the visit into an informal discussion about the course and the teaching in general, for your evaluation purposes. Sadly, we have less and less time to talk to students these days – so make the most of it.

Independent learning

Self-instruction

Learning has never been entirely dependent on teaching and teachers. Many people can and do study and learn subjects themselves, without the benefit of formal instruction by an accredited teacher. Indeed, when one considers the number of famous self-taught mathematicians, scientists and musicians, one begins to wonder about the need for teachers at all. Also, of course many people follow their personal interests and hobbies without formal instruction, becoming experts in pop music, football, motorcycle mechanics, politics (in which we are all born experts, of course) and so on. Correspondence colleges across the world produce 'teaching packages' and self-instructional material in a range of subjects. Vocational and professional in-service training is often based on teaching packages, and little else. The UK's Open University depends almost entirely on independent learning, enabling students to study very much what they like, where they like, to some extent at their own pace and in a manner which suits their own particular needs. So independent learning, open learning, self-instruction, distance education, resource-based learning or whatever you wish to call it, is a valid and effective means of teaching. I will refer to it as *open learning*, the open referring to the degree of freedom and flexibility which the learner has. There is a distinction between open learning at a distance, such as is conducted by the Open University, and on-site open learning. It is the latter which concerns us here, as this book is primarily about 'conventional' university teaching. But in either case there is the need for specially dedicated teaching materials, designed to make up for the reduced face-to-face teaching (Race,1989; Rowntree, 1990).

Support material for open learning

The support material for open learning in a conventional university must be more substantial than students might expect to receive on courses delivered by the formal lecture method. Typical characteristics of such material have been given in Chapter Three (page 40). However, this need not imply the lengthy preparation time normally associated with open learning materials (Ellington and Race, 1993), for three reasons. First, the *real* difficulty in preparing any course lies in getting across the crucial messages in the most effective and efficient manner – that is, producing the core of your notes. This you must do, no matter how you intend to present the material. Preparing the material for open learning presentation means a little more thought or more careful and expansive explanation to aid the independent student, providing her/him with regular self-assessment questions and other feedback. You have to anticipate what difficulties the student may have and provide ways to get out of them – you are not there to point out the ways round blockages. Second, people are far better at independent learning than teachers are apt to credit. Certainly, high-calibre university students should be able to learn independently from a good textbook. The idea of open learning is not to replace this, but to speed it up. Third, in a conventional university you can offer far more support and see much more of the students, who are therefore less dependent on the material. They also automatically receive and give support from/to their peers in the class.

The role of the teacher in open learning

The teacher using open learning methods has a somewhat different role from that in the formal lecture method. One may still provide a set of lectures, but generally these will be of a different type – summarizing and synthesizing a number of ideas and topics; targeting the particularly diffi-cult topics; preparing and motivating students for the next unit, etc. There will be less need to cover routine material. The teacher also fulfils the valuable role of counsellor and adviser; provides regular feedback and encouragement and deals with individual problems. Any lectures and tutorials should be much more a group and interactive activity.

Students involved in open learning are usually more demanding than conventional students. Having studied the material carefully themselves their feeling of ownership is greater and they will often pick up quite difficult points. They also expect similar commitment from you. Tutorial sessions with open learners can be very stimulating – and exhausting. Unfortunately, students often have different sticking points and are at different places in the course/unit and so it is difficult to provide a focus for a particular tutorial or lecture. In a conventional university you have greater contact and more control over this, so the problem should not be too great.

Flexibility of open learning

The open learning approach is particularly useful for certain types of courses, or parts of courses, including introductory material, regularly repeated and highly standard lectures, routine material, background material, prerequisites and preliminary material, optional material.

Certain types of students particularly benefit from an open learning approach. Clearly the very good students, capable of teaching themselves, may prefer to forego formal lectures. But weaker students may also value the opportunity to take a slower pace and spend more time on some aspects of their studies, rather than sleeping through meaningless lectures. Some students simply don't like formal teaching anyway and become alienated by it. Foreign students may find the fast delivery of a formal lecture incomprehensible and would prefer to have good hard copy course mate-rial available to study at their leisure. Shy, retiring and over-anxious students, intimidated by a formal classroom situation, may prefer to make their mistakes in private. Finally, it is much easier for students suffering from enforced absence by illness or late enrolment, for example, to catch up if the support material is available (they can even study in hospital).

Maintaining discipline in the classroom

Setting the rules of conduct

It is a mistake to believe that discipline is unnecessary in university teaching. Certainly it is less of a problem than at school level, but there can be difficulties you need to be aware of and be able to cope with effectively. You occasionally get the bad student or group of students who seem intent on disrupting proceedings – talking among themselves, caustic comments, persistent lateness. Many discipline problems can be created by the tutor, however, if he/she is not attentive enough to students' problems during lectures, or as a result of inadequate preparation or presentation.

Do not be bashful about demanding that the students conform to your wishes in the conduct of the class, particularly if you have already discussed these with them. You cannot demand respect or affection, they have to be earned, but you *can* demand and expect common courtesy and you must – on behalf of the class as a whole. So do not tolerate disruptive behaviour.

Dealing with disruption

If disruption occurs, locate the source and the cause of the problem. For instance, a general rumbling of muttering throughout the class, with many sighs and 'tut-tuts', invariably means you have transgressed. Perhaps you are writing too fast; someone cannot hear you; you have erased some material too quickly. Simply ask what the problem is and reiterate that you would appreciate quiet in the classroom, unless there is specific comment to be made. One reason for constantly looking at the class, rather than the board, is to detect problems early.

If some students continue to misbehave after your initial polite request, warn them that they will be asked to leave the class if they persist. If you can do this with humour (not sarcasm) so much the better, but the message must be firm and clear. Also, do not alienate the whole class by your warning – in fact, you should try and get them on your side (they usually will be) by pointing out that everyone suffers and precious time is being wasted as a result of disruption.

At the third offence, request the student(s) to leave. If they refuse, you leave and inform the appropriate course tutor, giving your reasons. The problem must be resolved one way or the other before the next lecture, so that the bulk of the students do not suffer unduly. Really, things should not get to this stage and, indeed, very rarely do. But abandoning the class is the only real sanction you have during the lesson and it is actually very effective – the offender(s) will be isolated and have no sympathy from the rest of the class. If this course of action does not appeal to you, formulate your own, ensuring it is robust and resolute enough to cope with the more difficult situations. Whatever you do, do not end up in an unseemly quarrel with the students – it just wastes time and resolves nothing.

Exercise control

There is often a temptation to let the class itself enforce its own discipline, relying on the responsible majority to quieten down the few disruptive students. You rarely have time for this – and you are, after all, the one in charge. In my experience the students have more respect for the teacher who demonstrates control over unruly elements in a classroom.

Do not try to compete with noise in the classroom by talking louder, for example. Why should you? Just insist on quiet and proper consideration. You should aim for a situation in which you can allow discussion and noise when it suits you, maybe a joke or two, but you can quieten the class down with a word or two when necessary. If students see that you are prepared to shout above their noise they will let you go on doing it. You can sometimes quieten a class down by simply standing, notes in hand, staring at one or two students for a few seconds, then commencing to lecture. If you do need to ask them to be quiet, make sure everyone can hear you – you may have to shout! Don't start writing or lecturing expecting the chatter to subside – it may do, but you are then allowing the students to dictate the terms.

In dealing with the students, be open, firm and fair. Respect them and try to be yourself with them. You have a professional relationship with them, but you also need to develop some personal rapport with them and the more you can relax and act naturally, the easier that should be. If a student annoys, offends or pleases you, show it – but gently and without malice or favour. You are not a talking, writing robot delivering information and you don't need to be. Should the need arise for disciplinary action, your position will be strengthened if it is seen as the outcome of a reasonable personal and professional response, rather than as an authoritarian imposition. Of course, you should always explain the reasons for your actions – this is a must when dealing with young adults.

A time-honoured technique for defusing a situation and neutralizing a troublesome student is to ask him/her to explain something on the board – in the nicest possible way, of course. The object is not to make a fool of the student, but to show him/her your difficulties. Just hope the student doesn't do a better job than you!

Always take time to consider decisions

Sometimes students make specific requests which put you on the spot and find you unsure how to respond. For example, they may ask for specimen solutions to last year's examination paper, when you had not intended to issue this. You may feel it unreasonable to refuse, especially when they tell you another teacher issues such solutions. On the other hand, the full implications may not be immediately obvious to you (perhaps you intended to recycle a question) and you feel uneasy about acceding without some thought. Well, don't. On such occasions, if you feel the slightest unease or discomfort, simply say you will think about it, do so, then get back with your considered response. This should be sufficiently reasonable to withstand the possible consequences. I labour this because it is precisely such incidents which cause a disproportionate amount of ill-feeling, controversy and stress in teaching. Never allow a student (or anyone else) to ambush you into a hasty decision.

Deadlines and absenteeism

A common problem with students arises from such things as late submission of coursework or assignments, where you always get the few who try to milk the system – and it is often the most likeable students. You have to be firm on such things as deadlines, simply out of fairness to the students who do submit on time. It is perfectly true that if you give them a centimetre they will take a kilometre – we all do. It is also very difficult to enforce such things strictly – you feel you are being unreasonable. However, the prime teaching function of coursework is to give quick feedback to the students and you cannot, for example, issue worked answers if there are outstanding submissions. Whenever you have difficulty enforcing rules, deadlines, etc. remember that your first priority should be one of fairness to the majority of the students. Of course, you should always be alert to the genuine case (not easy – the ingenious fabrications you will hear will soon make you sceptical of any excuse). Investigate such cases further to determine to what extent the student's problem affects their work generally. Sometimes a request for late submission can be a call for help in more ways than one. Whatever course of action you decide to adopt on this matter, be sure it is clear, consistent and well known to the students.

Absenteeism is another area to watch. The naïve belief that lectures/ tutorials are not compulsory is misguided. Some departments require satisfactory attendance before they will recommend continuation of grant awards, or they may inform a sponsor of a student's absenteeism. Some departments require a register to be taken. For the bulk of the students skipping an occasional lecture is no problem, but the thing to watch for is the prolonged absence of a student. There may be many reasons for such absence, but whatever it may be, it is your concern – up to a point. For small classes, in which you can easily keep track of students, you should be able to account for prolonged absenteeism. In very large classes this may go unnoticed and mechanisms for dealing with it will be a departmental or institutional responsibility.

Formal disciplinary and complaints procedures

There are a number of levels at which a student may be 'disciplined', from a stern word from the tutor, to withdrawal of registration by the university. Formal disciplining is such a rare occurrence that the only advice necessary is to consult a senior colleague, or your head of department, immediately you become involved in any such action.

Just as there are formal procedures for disciplining students, so there are mechanisms for students to make complaints about their course, your lecturing, or whatever – and there will generally be complaints about something in the system. Often, the students, or their representative will complain to their programme tutor, who will then relay it to his head of department, who contacts your head of department, who eventually gets to you. It saves everyone a lot of work if you can short circuit this process by having a good working relationship with the various programme tutors. More important, you should seek to establish a relationship with the class so that they will complain immediately and unhesitatingly to you directly. Problems between teacher and students should only be sorted out by third parties as a very last resort. Such open and direct relationships also greatly benefit the teaching and learning process.

'Collaboration'/cheating in student assessment

Students naturally collaborate when working on coursework and it is difficult to separate this from cheating. It is often impossible to decide who copied whom. Even though some of the students may be obtaining a few marks for little effort, this can be tolerated because the very act of working together is helpful to them. However, on occasions it can be obvious – down to identical mistakes. Initially, nothing more than a few words to the students concerned should be necessary. A warning shot in the form of a deliberately low identical mark is often quite effective. If the problem persists you should tell the students that the Board of Examiners for their course will be informed of the matter. Coursework is such a good teaching method that it is worth living with the minor disadvantages of its possible abuse – but we should try to minimize them.

The difficult class/student

There *is* such a thing as the 'difficult class' (as well as a 'good class'), where you just do not seem to hit it off. If the class is larger than about 30 students then it is more likely to be you that is the problem, since such a large cross-section will not usually give you a hard time for no reason. If you sense that there is something wrong, be frank and open with the students and discuss it with them. You may have to probe a little, but you should be able to tease an explanation out of some of the students. Often it will come down to simply a misunderstanding – perhaps you assumed a background knowledge they didn't have, for example.

In smaller classes you can have a situation where the disruptive nature of one or two individuals infects the whole class and generates an unpleasant atmosphere (the reverse of this is when you have one or two lively, intelligent characters who can put a buzz into the class and produce a great atmosphere). Again, you have to face up to this openly and frankly. Basically, you have to neutralize the influence of the trouble-makers by persuading the class to marginalize them, or remove their influence altogether. Whatever you do – don't put up with it.

Problems specific to you

Some staff may have special problems with discipline, due to their personal disposition or other factors. For example, a timid, quietly spoken teacher may have difficulty asserting authority over a hundred rowdy engineering students. If this applies to you, you must accept that it is an additional burden on you and that you will need to work harder in all aspects that have been noted above and apply more thought to your teaching. To boost your confidence, remember that you are in charge, you hold all the cards and you do not have to tolerate unreasonable behaviour. You need, as a matter of course, to ensure that your communication is effective – so use a microphone if necessary. Take some assertiveness training if you think it will help. Seek advice from colleagues, or head of department, as soon as possible and, if all else fails, ask for a change of course. I doubt that you will need to go that far.

Support from your colleagues

Don't be afraid to use more experienced and 'assertive' colleagues to assist you with problem students. You are not running and hiding behind someone else – you are fully utilizing the resources of the department. When I was at school, our prissy headmistress Miss Thompson had no scruples about using the plimsoll-wielding 'Basher Bill' as her enforcer when the need arose. Nobody messed with Miss Thompson. If you are having difficulties with a class and you can't locate the problem, you may find it helpful to ask an experienced colleague to sit in, discreetly. They will often spot the problem immediately and suggest remedies. Again, there is no shame in this – we must all learn, and the quicker we can do so, the better.

Personal involvement

Try to learn at least a fair proportion of the students' names (not easy in a class of 200). Just as in everyday life, how you address them is between yourselves. I favour 'Mr X' and 'Ms Y', simply because it is more specific, but first names are sometimes appropriate. It is difficult remembering names and you have to work at it – it helps if you meet socially, or in small tutorial groups. Knowing a fair selection of names is useful in controlling the class – students are less inclined to misbehave if they *think* you can identify them.

Avoid passing comment on the qualities or attributes of a third party, student or staff, with students. This is common courtesy in any human relationship, but we all moan about each other. The situation is different between you and students, however – keep it strictly professional. This advice is quite general so far as interaction with your students is concerned – any involvement which may compromise your professional relationship is to be avoided.

Chapter Five

Assessment and Feedback

Forms of assessment

Assessment is difficult – for the teacher too

Assessment is one of the most important parts of the teacher's job. This is the point at which you test the extent to which students have achieved the course objectives. It is a difficult and stressful procedure because you may have to make uncomfortable decisions about people you have grown to know and like. Also, it may call for a great deal of soul-searching on your own part. It is surprising (and comforting) how many teachers are unsure about what constitutes an appropriate 'standard' in their subject and how reluctant they are to blight a student's career by rigid adherence to such a vague notion. I am happy to say that in my experience, I have found that most teachers err on the side of caution and are usually willing to give students the benefit of any doubt.

Forms of assessment

The common forms of assessment are:

  – Coursework
  – Written examination (essay, multiple-choice, open-book)
  – Oral and aural examinations
  – Project work
  – Laboratory reports
  – Class tests and quizzes
  – Direct observation, as in clinical education

Increasingly, methods of self-, group- and peer-assessment are also being used.

The purpose of assessment

The purpose of assessment is not merely to frighten students into learning the course material. There are a number of equally laudable reasons for assessment. Mehrens and Lehmann (1984) give, as the purposes of assessment:

- To judge the extent to which the essential skills and knowledge have been mastered.
- To monitor improvement over time.
- To diagnose students' difficulties.
- To evaluate the teaching methods.
- To evaluate the effectiveness of the course.
- To 'motivate' students to study.

Some authors (Bligh *et al*, 1981) add to these the purpose of predicting future behaviour. It is a worrying paradox of assessment that this is the purpose for which most assessment methods are least suited, and yet it is the purpose for which they are most often used. It is precisely because of this long-term (life in some cases) use of the results of academic assessment that great care needs to be taken in making the assessment method as valid, reliable and fair as possible.

Administrative and organizational implications

Assessment imposes a considerable administrative and organizational burden on teachers and the university and substantial stress on the students. It is one of the major resource-consuming activities in the university calendar, in terms of academic and non-academic staff time (including, for example, counselling staff – for teachers as well as students!) and accommodation facilities. It is also one of the activities in which the academic's usual cavalier approach to university regulations has to be suspended for a more rigorous attention to the rules. There are a wide range of administrative, organizational and regulatory practices which vary from institution to institution. These concern the timetabling, accommodation, setting, administration, invigilation, marking and moderating of examinations and other assessment, culminating in consideration of the results by the appropriate *Examination Board*. Familiarize yourself with all aspects of this process which affect you and comply with the regulations scrupulously. Do all that you can to facilitate the assessment process and to ease the burden of those involved – prompt submission of examination papers and marks, responsible performance of invigilation duties, etc. It is tiresome, but vital.

Summative and formative assessment

There is a distinction between assessment designed to inform decisions on the student's future, such as sessional examinations, and assessment designed to diagnose student problems for the guidance of their subsequent study and assist in the learning process, such as diagnostic tests. The former is called *summative assessment*, the latter *formative assessment* – but of course some assessment, such as coursework, may have elements of both forms.

Clearly, everyone takes summative assessment much more seriously, although in terms of the learning process the formative kind is perhaps as important. Students should, of course, be told of the nature of any assessment to be used.

Coursework and continuous assessment

Coursework is as much about teaching as assessment. The assessment element provides motivation to assimilate course content as it is taught and allows students to spread their efforts and gain rewards over a longer time span. At the same time the students receive formative feedback to correct and consolidate their learning. The proportion of a unit of assessment devoted to continuous assessment as opposed to a final examination can vary widely, providing one of the more controversial issues of teaching. This is usually a departmental decision. It is important to provide feedback on coursework as quickly as possible, while the work done is fresh in the student's mind.

Given the contribution of continuous assessment to the overall unit of assessment for your course, it is still difficult to decide on the amount of coursework you should give. Seek guidance from colleagues on this (if you can get any agreement out of them). Some give regular, small amounts, others one large piece of work serving as revision near the end of the course. The standard of coursework cannot be too straightforward – there is something wrong if students regularly achieve 80–90 per cent in coursework and then scrape 40 per cent in the examination. It is useful if coursework is linked to key objectives of the course, providing reinforcement in essential topics and skills.

Norm- and criterion-referenced assessment

The 'measurement' aspect of assessment may be conveniently classified into two types. *Norm-referenced* assessment tends to use the results of all students to determine the standard used. That is, students are assessed in comparison with each other. Traditional examination practice relies on this sort of assessment, where the pass level of an examination is determined by the percentage of students given each grade. *Criterion-referenced* assessment determines the standard *a priori* before the examination, with the intention of ensuring certain minimal standards are met, or a minimal level of skill is acquired. Inevitably, some compromise in criterion-referenced assessment becomes necessary if too many students fail (or too many *pass*, in the case of some professional exams), but it does have the advantage that the objectivity and validity of the assessment is clear to everyone.

Open-book examinations

Some teachers favour open-book examinations, where the students have access to their notes or other reference material for the course. This has its merits, freeing students from relying on memory of every detail of the course. But it does call for a different type of examination question – more difficult, demanding more independent thinking from the student. As always, the best solution is probably a compromise, permitting the use of a 'handbook' or formula sheet containing limited or outline results from the course. Also, naturally, the form of the examination will reflect your general educational objectives. If you actually want students to recall and recognize certain items of information, then you can only test that facility by denying access to the information. Handbooks, formula sheets, etc. are sometimes used as props to help students through examinations for courses which contain too much material – this is bad practice.

Validity, reliability and practicality of assessment

Any assessment method used, whatever its purpose, must adhere to three requirements (Newble and Cannon, 1991):

- Validity – does it measure what it is supposed to?
- Reliability – are the results produced consistent?
- Practicality – is it practical in terms of time and resources?

Validity is determined by the matching of the objectives of the course to the assessment procedure. Reliability depends on the consistency of the assessment when, for example, it is applied to the same student at different times; or different people mark the same paper. Practicality depends on the availability of resources, the most crucial of which is *your* ability to assess in a prescribed time-scale.

Self- and peer-assessment

Self- and peer-assessment are very efficient means of carrying out formative, non-examinable assessment, but obviously require careful regulation for summative assessment purposes. Even if used for formative purposes, to provide feedback on progress for the teacher and students, for example, it is best to give it a formal status, so that the students take it seriously and it forms a well-defined component in the learning process. Of course, self- and peer-assessment are valuable in developing student ownership of the course material, involvement in it, independence and responsibility. It will also exercise their critical and evaluative skills.

Students will need training and guidance if they are to use self- and peer-assessment and it is best to introduce it gradually, using it initially only for formative assessment. They will need clear, explicitly stated criteria on which to base their judgements and must understand the need to justify their judgements and correlate them with those of their peers and the teacher. For routine, factually based or 'handle turning' questions, it should be sufficient for the teacher to provide a detailed specimen solution and marking scheme against which the student can compare their own or another's script. Then one must provide some safeguards as to the veracity of the marks produced – perhaps by the tutor marking a random sample of scripts and questions or double marking by the students. For deeper, more searching questions, such as essays, it is obviously much more difficult to guarantee the validity and reliability of student marking (or tutor marking for that matter!). You must provide a comprehensive list of general and specific criteria on which the student must comment on a scale which you make explicit to them. The use of essay self-assessment forms, on which students must justify their marking in great detail, provides one means of monitoring self- and peer-assessments (Gibbs, 1992b).

Group assessment

Particularly for large classes, assessment of students in groups is also quite efficient for formative assessment, but it needs rigorous safeguards if used for summative purposes. As with peer-assessment, assessing students in groups provides the opportunity to assess performance in the transferable skills such as teamwork and communication. Personally, I believe its summative use should be confined solely to these ends, rather than viewing it as a means of increasing efficiency.

Group assessment might appear to reduce the marking load on the teacher – marking 10 scripts produced by groups of 5 in a class of 50 *seems*, on the face of it to be easier than marking 50 individual scripts. However, there are considerable recurrent overheads in design of the questions, organization and training of the students and ensuring a fair distribution of the group mark among the group members. These overheads must be set against any saving in marking time. There is also no doubt that you lose valuable information about the performance of individual students which conventional assessment provides. In any case, the groups should not be too large (not more than about six students), limiting any efficiency gains.

As with self- and peer-assessment, students will need training in group working and its assessment. This alone will occupy you all for a couple of hours at least – how many scripts can you mark in that time and how much revision can the students do? If developing teamwork skills is one of the objectives of the course, fine, otherwise the benefits of group assessment are not so obvious. You will also need to devote time to explaining the assessment method and justifying its fairness to the students – and getting agreement on your approach.

The purpose of the group assessment may influence the method of distributing marks among the members of the group. Thus, if you wish to reward team work and overall effectiveness of the group then you might give every group member their total group mark. For more complicated objectives, considerable discussion and negotiation with the students may be involved both before and after assessment. Peer-assessment of the contribution of each group member is one way of providing a reasonably fair distribution of marks among the group (Gibbs, 1992b).

The students and assessment

I make no apologies for labouring the point that both the students and you must be clear, well in advance, about how your course is assessed and the percentage contributed to the final mark by each assessment component. Students should be informed, in writing, of all regulations pertinent to their assessment. Remember that most students take examinations very seriously so it is not a matter to be light-hearted about in discussions with them. Also, in so far as institutional policy permits, you should regard students' marks/ grades as private.

Students should have plenty of notice of the format of the examinations or other assessments, for example whether it is open-book, or multiple-choice. A specimen examination paper to illustrate the type and standard of questions is very helpful. Advance notice of the rubric should also be given, as well as details of what items may be used in the examination. For example, you may need to specify the type of calculator allowed.

Most students have plenty of training and experience in conventional examinations, but may be less familiar with oral examinations or project report writing. You may therefore need to provide them with practice in these and students generally benefit greatly from a mock oral presentation, or a preliminary discussion of a draft project.

There will inevitably be some student reaction following an examination, ranging from wide grins at an easy paper to scowls and maybe complaints to examination boards after a taxing paper. Be prepared for this and treat it seriously and sympathetically, even though your natural response might be to defend your position. Ensuring a clear link between course objectives and the examination questions will diffuse criticism about the content of the examination, but the most usual complaint is about the standard of the paper. I have never heard students complain that a paper was too easy. Consider any criticism objectively; consult colleagues; compare with past papers; check for errors in the paper. There may be formal procedures for appeals against coursework and examination marks, which you should follow to the letter.

Setting the examination

Examination questions

If you have a good problem bank then this will provide a ready supply of questions for examinations or coursework. Otherwise, construction of an examination from scratch can take a surprising amount of time, so allow for this. When you take on a course, ascertain its examination requirements as soon as possible – rough dates, length of paper, how many questions, is it shared, the rubric, etc.

Setting an examination question of the 'right' standard, which is fair and testing for the students is very difficult. As a guide you can consult past papers, elicit comments or suggestions from your colleagues and rely on internal and external moderation. The examination paper as a whole has got to test the students' knowledge and understanding of the course material and facility in the skills acquired. It must give the student opportunity to demonstrate both depth and breadth, so there must be questions ranging across the whole syllabus, with selected topics dealt with in some depth. It is helpful to give the available marks for each question on the examination paper.

A well-designed examination question should be linked to the central objectives of the course, with side issues playing a minor role. It should be at the appropriate standard, having clear, precise and unambiguous instructions and no nasty tricks. The questions should be linked to a comprehensive, complete marking scheme, which is applied identically to all candidates. It should be a reliable test of the abilities for which it is designed in that examiners marking independently agree closely on marks.

Easy to set – hard to mark

There is a crude inverse relation between ease of setting and ease of marking an examination question. Questions requiring little preparation to set, such as 'Write an essay on ...' are often very difficult to mark. On the other hand, *objective* or *multiple-choice* tests, which require simple choices or true/false type answers are very easy to mark, but require lengthy and careful preparation, especially if they are to be used for summative assessment purposes. When setting multiple-choice tests make sure all your choices are 'equally likely'. Such tests are most useful for rough and ready formative diagnostic tests. Choices of distractors (the wrong answers) can often be culled from previous class tests, coursework or examinations.

When setting essay-type questions, ensure that the students are familiar with the weighting given to different aspects such as content and presentation. Such questions test ability to organize, evaluate and think as much as they do content and substance. Students tend to prepare more fully for essay questions, enhancing their educational value.

It is often said that short or multiple-choice questions tend to assess and reinforce the surface approach to learning, while essay questions demand deep learning approaches. I have my doubts about this. Particularly in the scientific subjects it is quite straightforward to set multiple-choice tests which are extremely searching, while good marks may be obtained to some types of essay questions easily enough with a surface approach – list the main points and wrap waffle round them. It is more likely that the overloading of syllabuses and the decline in resources which has driven many teachers to adopt multiple-choice tests is the cause of surface approach learning, not the tests themselves.

An opportunity, not a trial

The objective of an examination is to find out what the student knows, not what they don't know. So the most helpful format for the student is one in which they can fulfil their potential by attempting as much material as possible, without fear that it will not be credited. It is difficult to justify forcing the student to choose between two alternatives, each of which they could do equally well. Try to find ways of extracting the best from the student.

A typical examination paper should contain reasonable proportions of routine and of more testing items. A fairly standard format for a question is to start with a gentle introductory bit of bookwork to give the student confidence, followed by a reasonably routine techniques or applications exercise, finishing the question with a tougher portion requiring skill and ingenuity. The question format and standard may depend on the type of student involved. Thus, a student taking a course as a subsidiary subject may be examined less rigorously than one taking the same course as a main subject. Generally, fit the format and difficulty to the students examined.

Format and duration

Format and typical examination duration vary from course to course. A short, 1-hour test may be suitable in some circumstances, a formal, 3-hour examination in others. The important thing is that the students know what to expect. Your colleagues will give you lots of ideas. Seek advice if you intend to deviate markedly from normal practice. Generally, the paper should include a wide selection of topics from the course, but should not give an excessive amount of choice.

Once you know the format of your paper and the rough question lengths, it is easier to put the questions together. Obviously a 30-minute question for the students may take you a fraction of that time and so it is difficult to judge the content of a question of specified duration for a given set of students. It is largely a matter of common sense and experience, but some rough guidelines are possible, depending on the subject. For example, in mathematics I work on roughly 2 to 3 pages for the solution to a 30-minute question, written out in the same style that I would expect from the students. You will be able to establish similar rough and ready rules of thumb from your own undergraduate experience and from discussion with colleagues and by working through past papers. Make sure your questions fit the syllabus and the notation and terminology used in the course notes – students get very indignant otherwise.

Rubric

The *rubric* is the set of instructions printed on the examination paper, which tells the students such things as how many questions to attempt and what materials and equipment such as graph paper, tables and calculators may be used. Make sure the rubric for the examination paper is explicit, comprehensive, clear and unambiguous. Throughout the year students will ask you about the examination format, what they are expected to do and even what the questions will be. On no account rely on verbal instructions in such matters – the rubric is the only official guide to how the students should tackle the examination. Any verbal information you give should simply reiterate the rubric.

Administrative considerations

There are deadlines for setting all examinations, but ideally you should anticipate these by as much as possible. You may find it difficult to set questions on material not yet covered, but on the other hand, once the questions are set you know what the course is aiming at.

Moderation of the examination

Particularly in the early stages of your teaching career, ask colleagues to have a glance at your examinations to check that you have it broadly right. Your department may have a policy of formal moderation. In some cases papers may be seen by an external examiner, so there are a number of ways you can get feedback on your examination papers.

Avoid the predictable examination

After the first year of your course the going is easier, you have a pattern to work from. Within a few years you may be reduced to recycling questions – we all run out of ideas eventually. The situation to avoid is that when the examination becomes predictable and question-spotting a formality. The examination then gets easier and your results increasingly impressive. Then you have to make an effort to change the pattern of the paper – but do not change things quickly and drastically, taking the students by surprise, or you will have high failure rates to explain.

Marking the examination/coursework

Marking-time

This is when you really find out how much the students have learnt from you – don't take it too hard. At least the more ludicrous mistakes provide good stories for the coffee room (no names, of course). Marking-time is an intensive and stressful part of the academic year for most teachers. It uses up a lot of nervous energy, so be prepared for it. Careful thought in setting the paper, a good comprehensive set of specimen solutions and marking schemes will ease the burden. Also useful is an awareness of the sort of errors students can make. But nothing quite prepares you for the gruelling task of wading through paper after paper, trying to maintain concentration and patience. You may prefer to split the marking into shorter intense sessions, although sometimes the marks are required so quickly you have to slog on through the night. My family prefer the latter – then they don't have to be around me when I am doing it!

It is often best to mark all attempts at each question at the same time, so that you become fully familiar with the (sometimes unsuspected) intricacies of the solution and the possible errors students can make. When doing this you may find that your ideas change throughout the marking and you may need to backtrack. On the other hand, particularly for short questions, you can often go very quickly through a whole paper at one go. An advantage of marking a question at a time is that you are less influenced by the student's performance in other questions.

The reliability of your marking can be improved by marking questions without knowledge of the candidate's name. Indeed, in the interests of fairness, many universities now have a general policy of anonymous marking, and there is little doubt that students favour this. Another means of improving the reliability of your marking is to shuffle the scripts between marking each question. Also try not to be influenced unduly by handwriting or other presentational aspects unrelated to competence in the subject of the examination. If you have to mark in more than one sitting, reread papers previously marked to maintain consistent marking standards. Certainly, if you have a large number of scripts to mark, it is worthwhile choosing a few as typical models of different grades so that you can regularly refer back to them to maintain a consistent standard.

Examination marking is definitely a topic on which to consult with your colleagues. A chat with a sympathetic, experienced teacher, working through a few scripts, can be just the thing. As with most aspects of teaching, you will soon discover that even experienced teachers have different views on examination marking, so sift through the advice and draw your own conclusions.

Follow errors through

Do not penalize students more than once for the same error – carry the error through the question and give full marks for subsequent sections which are correct, even if use is made of the erroneous results. Try to be generous and give the benefit of the doubt, without compromising standards.

Marking essays

Essay-type questions are arduous to mark. They are also prone to highly subjective judgement by the marker. There is a wealth of evidence that different people marking the same essay can produce widely varying results and care must be taken to minimize this effect. Essay questions, and others having a significant subjective component, are often marked within the context of what psychologists call the 'single stimulus situation' (McKeachie, 1978). Here, the marker grades the first-read papers relatively objectively against some absolute standard, which is deemed appropriate. But then subsequent papers are marked within the frame of reference set by the initial papers. Because most people tend to relax their standards and become more generous as they work through papers, the earlier marked papers then tend to be graded more severely than later ones. Then you may have to go back and re-read the earlier papers. This effect can be minimized by quickly reading through *all* the papers before you commence marking, thereby establishing a rough idea of what the general attainment is. Ranking the solutions in approximate order of merit before detailed marking helps too. You can also minimize the subjective element by having a precise list of points the answers should address and then establishing bounds on the marks for these points, depending on the other objectives you wish to achieve. Thus, you might expect say, ten points to be mentioned, three of which require wide and deep treatment, thereby attracting higher marks, while the other points require less attention. Then you will want some marks set aside for overall presentation, organization, clarity, consistency. Examinations having a significant subjective element should ideally be assessed by more than one examiner, ie monitoring of marking, or double marking.

Marking multiple-choice tests

Multiple-choice tests are particularly easy to mark, but usually give a blunter assessment of the students' abilities. They can even be marked by non-experts, or automatically. This is standard practice in the USA and Canada, where computerized marking by optical scanner is commonplace. The complete process of marking, recording and analysis of results, feedback and advice can be computerized, freeing the tutor to devote more time to dealing with students' difficulties detected by the tests. Multiple-choice tests are particularly useful for diagnostic purposes. From the quick results which they yield, you can home in on areas needing further treatment and can design more searching assessment in these, by written examination, for example. On the other hand, it is often very informative to mark such tests yourself, particularly if a few open-ended questions have been included, and students also submit their calculations. Then you can fly through the correct responses but, if need be, you can dig more deeply into the errors there and then. This is efficient and effective even for large classes.

Moderation in marking

A common mistake is to go into too much detail in marking and take it *too* seriously. This seems to conflict with the exhortation to treat examinations as seriously as do the students, but provided you are fair and give reasonable benefit of the doubt, you can afford to be less than meticulous in marking. The point is that examinations are such a crude instrument in any case (but probably the best we have) – how can you be so certain that your questions provide a precise and fair measure of the students' abilities? Again, common sense is the key – there seems little profit in anguishing over whether or not to award a half mark or a whole mark, in a question attracting 25 marks, for example. If in doubt – award 1.

Be prepared to modify your views on the difficulty of a question on marking it. It is not easy to judge how difficult the students will find a piece of work and if a large number of students have done very badly/well on a particular question then it's safe to assume that it was perhaps a little hard/easy. So you may realign your marking scheme in the light of this, although be in less of a hurry to take marks off rather than add them.

Standards and attrition rates

When all the marking is done, go through the results and have another look at any borderline cases. If the pass mark is 40 per cent, there will be a few raised eyebrows at the Examination Board if you offer a number of 39 per cents – no one can claim this accuracy for their marking and a bit of common sense is needed. On this point, it is worth noting that the 40 per cent passmark seems a peculiarly British tradition, 50 per cent being closer to the norm in many countries. There is in fact a lot to be said for the higher pass mark since variations about it are proportionately less sensitive to unreliable marking.

There is no doubt that in the future, as part of assessment of the quality of teaching, close attention will be paid to attrition rates of courses. So look at your failure rates carefully. Using 'declining standards', mixed classes, under-resourcing and the like to excuse failure rates of 40 or 50 per cent is not on. High failure rates are telling you something is wrong and you need to find out what it is. Some courses are notoriously difficult by their very nature – mathematics and dynamics often give first-year engineers unusual difficulties, for example – but at worst, this should be reflected in lower averages, not high failure rates. The course structure may be wrong; the syllabus too heavy; the parent department may hold the subject in low regard (students get to know such things); the level may have been pitched too high; incorrect assumptions about background may have been made, and so on. Whatever it is, high failure rates are not the sole responsibility of the students and it is the teacher's job to find out what is going wrong and correct it. The alarm bells should start ringing at anything above 10 per cent failure rate.

On the other hand, you must maintain standards. If the word gets around that you will automatically scale the mark to ensure a respectable pass rate, you can guess what will happen. In my view this is less of a problem than some believe. The general student body wishes to maintain standards – they don't want their degrees devalued and are prepared to do a fair day's work to obtain a good examination result. However, this must be attainable within the context of their academic history, the time and facilities available to them. High failure rates are often an indication that the structure, content, or teaching of the course has not kept pace with developments further up the line and the student's task has simply become too much. You may be able to set just as tough an examination on a different mix of topics and yet still achieve a respectable pass rate.

In your early teaching years you may try to head off such problems by setting a mock test/examination, which will also help the students with their revision. Remember, however, that even if you have time for this, the students may not. Setting a specimen examination paper as coursework is an effective compromise.

Errors in the examination paper

If, during the examination, you find a mistake in a question, correct it there and then, ensuring that all students are informed of the error. Make allowance for this when marking. If you discover an error only upon coming to mark the scripts then you need to decide whether to zero weight that part of the question, award something to people who have attempted it, or take other action. In any event, all such errors should be reported to the Examination Board, along with your treatment of them.

Reporting of results

The Examination Board

What happens to the assessment results after marking? If you don't know, find out as soon as possible. The results may disappear into an administrative black box with which you have no further dealings, or they may simply be between you and the students, in the case of formative assessment. However, for most summative assessment purposes the marks will be collated and considered, along with those from the students' other subjects, by an *Examination Board*, of which you will probably be a member. The Board will usually comprise all relevant examiners, possibly one or more external examiners and various other folk. The composition, powers and remit of such a board will be embodied in the institution's regulations. There will be an administrative and organizational structure associated with the Board's function and there will be a timetable for such things as examination times, submission dates for results, dates of Board meetings, appeals and informing students of the results. Someone, somewhere in your institution knows all about this and is responsible for its smooth working. Track them down and ascertain your role in the proceedings. In a perfect world, most of this will be arranged automatically and all you will need to do is note dates in your diary and stick to them, anticipating all your deadlines. In the increasingly 'real' world, hiccups occur. Recently I had one board reconvened because the first meeting lacked a quorum and I know of tutors failing to deliver results in time for Examination Boards. I am sure everyone shares such experiences and that due to under-resourcing and other pressures, they are becoming more frequent. We must all try to avoid such problems *but*, more important, when they do arise we must ensure that the reasons for them are fully understood – we must not be held culpable for under-resourcing.

Always keep a copy of your crude submitted marks and check them off with the Examination Board copy. Have the scripts available for consultation at the Board (usually, all this will be arranged for you). Do not be intimidated by the ranks of more experienced and senior staff at the Examination Board. You only have to listen to the arguments raging between them for a few minutes to realize that you may have something equally valuable to contribute. Your main priority should be to ensure fair play for the students, in the context of maintaining acceptable standards. In fact, everyone there will share this view – except that opinion will differ as to how it should be achieved. You can report to the Board any relevant information about the student(s), which may have affected their performance, but always be objective about this.

Decisions by the Examination Board

In practice, Examination Board discussions revolve around the borderline cases, those well within the classification bounds needing less attention. So be well briefed on such cases – recheck their scripts, look at any other material available such as coursework marks and previous years' results.

The Examination Board will decide on such matters as whether a student should be referred, or asked to withdraw. Guidelines for their actions are given in the appropriate regulations (of which most members of the Board are usually blissfully ignorant – an easy way to impress/bore your colleagues is to have a thorough knowledge of the regulations) but these still leave the Board plenty of latitude to make their own decisions. The most unwelcome outcome of such deliberations is the dreaded referred paper, which gives you one more job to do, just when you thought the course was finished.

Combining sub-assessments

Sometimes you may have to give a final assessment mark comprised of a number of sub-assessments (eg coursework + lab work + examination). Be careful how you combine such assessments – be wary of simple addition or averaging. There may be a department policy to guide you and you should certainly consult with colleagues if you have any doubts. The usual procedure is to convert each raw sub-assessment mark to a standardized score, suitable for averaging across the different assessment methods.

Feedback on coursework and continuous assessment

Opportunity for feedback

Coursework or continuous assessment provides the best opportunity for feedback on what students are learning from your course and also for reinforcing your teaching by individual positive comment and correction on the students' performance. Your comments should not only draw attention to errors on the script, but should praise good work such as the appropriateness of techniques used, clear logical exposition, and any evidence of flair and imagination. But do not be too free with your praise, lest you devalue it.

Marking for positive feedback

Give constructive criticism in a friendly and sympathetic tone, making it clear that it is the student's work which is being criticized and not the student. Never criticize without explaining the error and pointing out what the correct version should be. Point out inappropriate notation and terminology. Deficiencies in presentation and style are less serious, but the student should be made aware that these things do matter. If a solution is incomplete or inadequate, then explain what is missing. In fact a common failing among students (and teachers) is to labour a point, and on such occasions you will need to guide the student to a more succinct form of solution. If permitted by the regulations, indicate marks awarded section by section, explaining how they have been awarded (eg for accuracy, method, presentation, etc.). Show how the marks could be improved. Respond appropriately in obvious cases of copying and collusion.

Raise teaching points

Refer to appropriate sections of the course notes in your discussion of the students' errors, and indicate any revision that you think they need to do. Ask leading questions, and encourage the students to follow up any important points raised by the question or their solution. Where appropriate show how the students can check their own work, without relying on you to point out the errors. Indeed, vigorous self-criticism is an important adjunct to effective learning, and students should be encouraged to exercise it.

Offer support

Offer support to students who are obviously struggling. If a student's work is improving over past submissions, congratulate them. Direct students to other means of getting help (attending lectures and tutorials would be a start, but don't expect miracles). Provide model answers whenever appropriate.

Chapter Six

Evaluation of the Quality of Teaching

Introduction

'Evaluation', 'quality'?

Neither 'evaluation' nor 'quality' are currently well-defined, universally accepted terms in university teaching. Evaluation may refer to anything from the normal everyday formative feedback and self-criticism which teachers tend to do automatically, to the rigorous summative teacher assessment used in some institutions and countries to inform decisions on promotion, performance related pay and tenure. In North America 'evaluation' also refers to the assessment of students. Quality is also difficult to pin down in teaching. It may be viewed from the different perspectives of a range of stakeholders: students, teachers, institutions, employers, government, public and so on. It is also multi-dimensional, depending on the range of purposes attributed to the teaching and its outcomes by each of the stakeholders. It follows that any discussion of the evaluation of the quality of teaching will be contentious, at best. I will try to make my points clearly, so that you at least know what it is you are disagreeing with.

Accountability and efficiency

This chapter and the next relate to recent dramatic changes in higher education, which are occurring on a global scale (although at different rates and to varying degrees). Broadly these may be described as moves towards increased *accountability* (Chapter Six) and increased *efficiency* (Chapter Seven). I do not want to become enmeshed in the fine details of these developments. Both are moving so quickly and their impact differs from one country/institution to another to such an extent, that anything written becomes dated and parochial before the ink is dry. I doubt that the practising teacher has time to take much interest in such details in any case. (For those of you who *are* interested in the accountability issue, I can recommend: Coate, 1990; Ellis, 1993; Harvey *et al*, 1992; Her Majesty's Inspectorate, 1991; Higher Education Council, 1992 and Loder, 1990.) I will concentrate on the broad implications of these trends for the individual university teacher, and discuss how we may respond to them.

A lost opportunity?

I am well aware of how many teaching staff respond to the accountability trend – with mixtures of distrust, derision, cynicism and dismissiveness. In view of the way many countries are introducing accountability into the university sector, this is understandable. I have checked in an old dictionary and confirmed my suspicion that the word 'quality' actually predates the 1980s. One would not think so to judge from the way it is currently bandied about by governments and the civil service in the context of education in general and higher education in particular. It is as though we have never concerned ourselves with quality in our teaching; we have never cared for our students (sorry, 'customers'); we have never sought the views of employers about our graduates. We do not recognise 'quality' when we see it and we can only be persuaded to strive for it by abolishing tenure, having short-term contracts, performance-related pay and appraisal. We have to be assessed in teaching so that governments can point to bad teaching as a reason for reducing resources (use of norm-referenced criteria ensures this), while we are rarely trained in teaching, because this would require additional resources. Is it any wonder that appraisal, teaching-quality assessment, staff development and the like are viewed with suspicion and scepticism by many university teachers? In my view, the very real benefits which evaluation of teaching and staff development can bring to us all as practising teachers, have been dissipated by the inept and hasty manner in which they have been introduced in some countries, and the UK in particular. Teaching is a collegial and cooperative activity and the implementation of many recent reforms has done nothing but undermine these essential characteristics. Here, I will try to put aside these administrative and managerial bunglings and take an objective view of the positive aspects of the evaluation of teaching and its implications for staff development.

All around the world – accountability

The move towards greater accountability is a global one. Indeed '... the 1990s can already be characterised as the decade with an emphasis on the quality of higher education around the world' (Higher Education Council, 1992). In the USA higher education institutions are accredited both nationally and, subject by subject, by the various professional bodies. Funding is dependent on accreditation, which is largely effected by self-regulation and peer review (Her Majesty's Inspectorate, 1991). In recent years public concern has risen (or been raised?) about output performance from the higher education system and increased accountability is now demanded. At the same time resources have been eroded, resulting in greater use of non-tenure track appointments and short-term contracts (Deneef *et al*, 1988). In Britain higher education has shared the scrutiny to which all public services have been subjected, resulting in severe cut-backs in real resourcing and a dramatically increased accountability culture. Tenure has been abolished; short-term contracts are the norm; quality audit compels universities to do what they say they are doing; quality assessment links teaching to funding; research selectivity links research to funding; the Students' Charter (what about a Teachers' Charter?) will claim to give students greater say in their education; appraisal and performance-related pay will give academics less say (toe the line or your increments will get discretioned away). Similar moves are afoot, at various stages of development, across the EC (Brenman *et al*, 1992). Australia has gone down much the same path as Britain, although the approach there seems more enlightened than the UK fiasco (Higher Education Council, 1992) So, if you are a beleaguered academic, busily trying to get a paper off to the publisher before your appraisal tomorrow, when you just know your head of department is going to ask you to attend to dozens of forms relating to the impending Quality Audit, not to mention the not too distant Quality Assessment teaching inspection (don't mix the forms up – or does it matter?) – and you have just remembered you should have been in a class 15 minutes ago – YOU ARE NOT ALONE!

Accountability is good for the university teaching 'profession'

Regardless of the reasons for the move towards greater accountability, or the method by which this is achieved, there are good, positive reasons for embracing it. There are examples of poor teaching in universities (as there are examples of poor practice in every walk of life) and there is no doubt that teaching has been both undervalued and under-rewarded in higher education. It really is a scandal that university teachers receive no training in teaching – it is even more of a scandal that we are blamed for that fact. The absence of training in teaching has, perhaps rightly, enabled the claim to be made that university teaching is not a *profession*. It is therefore in our interests to jump on the accountability bandwagon, to help steer it towards the training needs of university teachers.

Formative evaluation as a basis for summative assessment of teaching

Recognition of good teaching is only possible if we know how to evaluate teaching. There is little agreement on how this is to be done. It is difficult to say, for example, how quality assessment of university teaching in Britain will impinge on the individual teacher. Inspectors will survey students, peruse their work and courseware and will make classroom observations – but more than this, we are unsure of the details. In this book I will take the view that, so far as the practising teacher is concerned, simple formative evaluation of teaching, and its systematic documentation by the teacher will form a sound basis for response to any formal summative assessment of teacher performance which may emerge.

What do we do ?

Before looking at the evaluation of teaching, it is worth considering teaching in the context of the full set of duties of a typical university teacher – *teaching, scholarship, research* and *administration*. Apart from you, the two other immediate stakeholders in your activities are the students and your institution. As you are probably aware, these groups have conflicting priorities. Understandably, students place the greatest value on your teaching function, while your institution may be more concerned with your research capability. The next section looks at the role of the university teacher from these different perspectives.

What the university teacher does

How students see the role of the university teacher

First we ask what the *students* expect of us. Key work on this was done by Startup (1972) in the USA, in the late 1960s, and the results are probably still valid today. Startup identifies 24 activities in which a typical teacher may be engaged which may be grouped into six categories, depending on the clientele involved, the objectives of the activity and the skills involved. The categories are:

A   Activities involving contact with undergraduates (four)
B   Activities associated with teaching (eight)
C   Research (one)
D   Postgraduate supervision (one)
E   Professional activities (five)
F   Administrative activities (five)

It was found that students regard activities relating to undergraduate teaching most highly. Also they give greater weight to small-group teaching than to lecturing. Research is secondary in importance, while administration ranks lowest. Remember that students do not *see* much of what you do – few of them can appreciate your research activity, or exercise value judgement on it.

Anecdotal evidence is always questionable, but some of the observations made by the students in Startup's survey give a clear insight into what they perceive as the role of the teacher and the primary function of an academic. I think you will agree that these comments are no less apposite today – and probably will be in another 20 years.

> *Professors and the senior lecturing staff should have all their purely administrative duties done by some official so they can concentrate on their various academic works.* (They should be so lucky.)

Student numbers should be cut drastically until sufficient staff and facilities are available for the degree of personal supervision which is essential to such a relatively high level of education. (Try telling that to the funding organizations.)

On how competently teachers fulfil their teaching role:

My impression of lectures is that lecturers are churning out the same rubbish year after year ... In most lectures all one can do is write and look it up after, nobody tries to understand; frankly I don't think the lecturers really care anyway. (It is sad, but some don't.)

The selection of staff should depend as much on their ability to impart knowledge in an interesting way, as on qualifications. (But how do you measure that?)

I would agree with the P. I. B. that students should have some influence on their lecturers' salaries since there is very poor feedback to bad lecturers. (Can lecturers have some influence on students' grants?)

All lecturers should attend a compulsory course in 'How to lecture properly – clearly and concisely'. This might improve the abysmal standard of lecturing of some staff. (Yes, it might.)

My parenthetical asides are irony, not sarcasm. I agree with much of what they say but regret that our paymasters do not.

Few experienced academics will be surprised by Startup's survey. Most will agree with the students' views and be sympathetic and understanding of their naïvety – their government will never pay for what they want, and neither will they when they have gone on to become lawyers and accountants and start to resent every penny/dime they pay in tax. In Britain, the Students' Charter gives students the forum to air their complaints – will anyone really listen? In the USA students have frequent opportunity to evaluate teaching – does anyone really listen? I think students will find that the only people who really listen to them are in the same boat with them – their teachers.

How the university sees the role of the university teacher

What do *you* think your institution sees as your role? I know – they want you to publish and pretty damned quick! This is not surprising. Often a significant proportion of funding is linked to research output. Further, research reputation has always been the main, if only, measure of academic worth in higher education. Many university teachers share complicity in this conspiracy, which manages to marginalize that for which we receive the bulk of our funding – teaching. Let's face it, much so-called research is in reality mediocre, hack development work, clinging to the coat-tails of real research which represents the highest achievements of the intellect. It is debatable whether this routine paper production is more intellectually respectable than good scholarship and teaching – start your colleagues off on that one and watch the sparks fly. Research is important, but as appointment, tenure, promotion and career advancement generally are invariably judged solely on research output, it is not heretical to ask if the balance is really right.

Most institutions, of course, are well aware of the tension between their priorities and those of the students and, as in all civilized communities, a sensible balance is aspired to and has largely been achieved in the past. It is increasingly difficult to maintain this. A department intent on raising its research income may appoint staff solely to do research, thereby increasing the teaching load on the remaining staff (if they let it) and possibly lowering teaching quality. In some institutions and countries it is not too strong to say that higher education has become a battleground between teaching and research interests – this cannot be good for either.

Quality in Higher Education project

Plainly, universities and their students sometimes have conflicting priorities – you, the teacher, are in the middle. We need a referee – or at least a more objective view. The Quality in Higher Education project sponsored by a partnership of education, government and business (Harvey *et al*, 1992), with the purpose of developing a methodology for assessing quality in higher education in Britain, attempts to provide this. The project sought the views of employers, students, academics, government, funding agencies and quality assessors and assurers on the criteria of quality by which higher education might be judged. The project found that the following 10 items were endorsed as a priority by at least four stakeholder groups.

- There are adequate physical resources (library, workshop, IT) to support teaching and learning.
- There are adequate human resources to support teaching and learning (and staff are properly qualified).
- The programme has clear aims and objectives which are understood by staff and students.
- The subject content relates to the programme's aims and objectives.
- Students are encouraged to be actively involved in, and given responsibility for, learning.
- The standard of the programme is appropriate to the award.
- Assessment is valid, objective and fair.
- Assessment covers the full range of course aims and objectives.
- Students receive useful feedback from assessment (and are kept informed of progress).
- Students leave with transferable knowledge and skills.

It appears that while there is a consensus about the importance of teaching, research is not regarded as a high priority. Research only ranked as a key criterion among quality assurers, and then only in as much as it supported teaching – blue-sky research didn't rate with anyone. Perhaps institutions should think more carefully about the teaching/research balance? They may be able to sustain the view that research is important, but they will not be able to get away with regarding teaching as any less important.

What does it mean for you?

Every university teacher must weigh the sometimes conflicting priorities referred to above, and decide his/her commitment to teaching relative to other duties. Then how will your teaching performance be evaluated and how might it be improved? How do you evaluate your own teaching? How do you know you are doing a good job? How would you justify what you do? How do you document your teaching activity? This chapter is devoted to these sorts of personal questions, rather than institutional matters.

What kind of evaluation of teaching?

Terminology

I use 'manager' in the following because I don't think any academics should see themselves as being managed. There are many who would like to see our vice chancellors as chief executives, presiding over a hierarchical line management – but I don't think we should oblige them. We really need another term which does not have the usual superior and supervisory connotations of 'manager', which are inappropriate in an academic context.

As yet there does not appear to be universal agreement about the terminology for evaluation/assessment of teaching. The problem is that evaluation is done for a number of different purposes by a number of different stakeholders, within and between institutions, and it is important to distinguish the various types of evaluation and assessment. These might be crudely categorized under *evaluation* (formative, done by practitioners for practitioners), *assessment* (summative, done by 'managers' for departmental or institutional objectives), and *appraisal* (formative, done by 'managers' for practitioners). The distinction between these types of evaluation is not helped by the fact that the titles used have the same dictionary meaning. Despite being an entirely inappropriate label, appraisal is, at least in the UK and Australia, a fairly widely accepted term for a definite managerial function in education. There is, however, confusion over the use of evaluation and assessment in reference to teaching, these terms being used either interchangeably or comprehensively by different authors. Here I will adopt the terminology of Ramsden and Dodds (1989), which seems to be precise and suitable for use by the practising teacher. This terminology recognizes the three distinct purposes for which an institution and its staff investigate the teaching activity:

EVALUATION of courses and teaching, by teachers, with a view to improvement – 'bottom up'.
APPRAISAL of (teaching) personnel, by 'managers' with the main objective of improving their performance – 'top down'.
PERFORMANCE ASSESSMENT, by 'managers', of the standard of teaching, or of

course provision in general, for the purpose of informing decisions on pay, promotion and so on - 'top down'.

Evaluation

Evaluation is used here to refer to the process of measuring the effects of a course or curriculum, its teaching and the student assessment on the students' learning, solely for the purposes of improving the course and teaching. It is something which most teaching staff are used to doing as part of the teaching process. It is done in a collegial manner, with self- and peer-assessment by teachers. The prime objective is the personal development of teaching skills and improvement of courses. Evaluation is done for and by the experts – the teachers themselves. *Formative evaluation* is that intended for diagnostic purposes, to uncover strengths and weaknesses, so that learning, teaching and courses may be improved. *Summative evaluation* is judgemental, with the main objective being to determine whether or not a particular standard has been attained.

Appraisal

It is sad that in some universities the purposes and ethos of appraisal are misunderstood. The trouble is, it is the wrong word – 'appraise' = estimate amount or worth of (Oxford English Dictionary). This is not even half the intended function of staff appraisal. Appraisal is a managerial process for assisting staff to improve their performance by confidential analysis, counselling and support. It should be interactive, with regular discussions between appraiser and appraisee and involve goal-setting and feedback on achievement of goals. The tragedy is that appraisal is sometimes viewed as a punitive process, primarily aimed at rooting out the backsliders. It is little wonder that appraisal is often regarded with suspicion by many academics. An effective appraisal scheme is about encouragement and inspiration, not censure.

Universities are democratic institutions *par excellence*. Your academic colleagues do not 'manage' you, whatever their seniority. Even though your appraiser may be of senior rank to yourself (and this is not always the case), there is no guarantee at all that he is a better teacher, researcher, or whatever. Also, of course, the appraisal process is concerned not solely with teaching, but the entire academic spectrum of teaching, research, scholarship and administration. Your appraiser may have little experience of or regard for teaching. Then, you either remain content to use your appraiser as a sounding board and honest broker – or you get yourself another appraiser. Whatever you do, please, for the good of the profession, don't acquiesce in a process in which teaching becomes a subject of 'managerial' prescription.

Performance assessment

Performance assessment refers to the managerial process of deciding whether a particular standard has been reached. Like student assessment, performance assessment of teachers, or teaching units, is a competitive process, with stick and carrot incentives (almost totally stick these days, it seems!). It is quite distinct from evaluation as defined above.

Performance assessment is done by 'managers' to determine whether a member of staff has achieved or is maintaining a particular standard. It is essentially summative, rather than diagnostic. As Ramsden and Dodds observe (1989) it has limited value in education because it is so difficult to measure the product of teaching. This will, of course, not deter its use by some university 'managements'. In the UK, the higher education funding councils speak of 'quality assessment' of teaching in precisely the sense we are using here – a university department's quality of teaching may be assessed as unsatisfactory, satisfactory or excellent, with consequences for funding hanging on the result.

Build on good evaluation

Of course, there are obvious overlaps in evaluation, performance assessment and appraisal, results of one feeding into the others, one providing motivation for the other and so on. While the purposes and outcomes of each are different (improved courses and teaching from evaluation; possible promotion from performance assessment; resources/training from appraisal), there is no need to regard them as mutually exclusive, resulting in repetition of effort, preparation and documentation. After all, all the processes are really aiming for the same ends – better courses and teaching – by different means. Since appraisal and performance assessment are likely to be based on institutionally centred criteria, I will concentrate on evaluation, on which you can build your response to appraisal and performance assessment. It is important to reiterate that good teachers have always, automatically, evaluated their teaching – the difference now is that appraisal and performance assessment have been introduced, across the system, in every activity, to formalize and 'top-down' the evaluation (appraisal) and to standardize and reward/penalize its outcome (performance assessment). What teachers have to do is to adapt the conduct and recording of evaluation to suit these new requirements – it is no longer sufficient to *do* it, you must now *tell* people you are doing it and *justify* the process and its outcomes.

Evaluation of teaching

How is teaching evaluated?

There is a wealth of literature on evaluation of teaching in primary and secondary education and no doubt much of this may be relevant to tertiary education. Also, evaluation of teaching in higher education has had a long history in some countries, notably the USA and Canada (Dressel, 1976; Hildebrand et al, 1971). There is less of a tradition of evaluation in Australia and Europe, but some good practical guidance has appeared in recent years (Gibbs *et al.*, 1989; Ramsden and Dodds, 1989; Partington, 1993), suitable for the practising teacher.

This chapter may seem unduly lengthy compared to others. This comes about because much of it consists of checklists which summarize good practice in all aspects of teaching considered in earlier chapters. Indeed, the teacher in a hurry may start with the checklists, digging deeper later on.

The purpose and methodology of evaluation of teaching depends on who is doing the evaluating. But all such evaluation will contain the same basic components, namely performance indicators, self-assessment and visitation/observation by experts and stakeholders. Here we are concerned solely with the evaluation, by a teacher, of his/her own teaching of a particular course, for the purposes of improving and developing that course and its teaching. This involves investigation of all aspects of the teaching activity, and may be conveniently built around the framework of Figure 1.

The basis of good evaluation

Ramsden (1992) sets down nine premises, with which I think most teachers would agree, on which good evaluation of teaching should be based. Briefly:

- Evaluation is about determining the view that students, you and others take of your courses and teaching.
- It is a multi-dimensional process, requiring input from many sources – students, your colleagues and others.
- It requires high quality and accurate interpretation prior to any action.
- The main aim is to uncover problems, rather than boost your ego.
- Evaluation is an essential part of teaching and mainly the responsibility of the teacher.
- It is a continuous and continuing process, providing feedback throughout the course.
- Evaluation is a collegial and cooperative activity – done by all teachers, for all teachers.
- Evaluation methods should hold no threat and should encourage teachers to show their strengths and weaknesses without prejudice.
- The method of evaluation is less important than the motivation to do it and regard for these nine premises.

Evaluation is expensive

Valid, reliable evaluation is difficult, costly and requires some commitment of time (I have heard 20 per cent of course time mentioned, but few can afford this without a corresponding increase in resources). One of the major impediments to the development of an evaluation culture in today's hard-pressed universities is the daunting array of methods hawked about by the enthusiastic evaluators. Only you can decide how much effort you can put into evaluation, and, having done so, which methods can meet your needs cost-effectively. You may also wish to enlist your colleagues' help with your evaluation, in which case you can reciprocate and share your findings and experience with them. Do not allow inappropriate, under-resourced or poorly designed evaluation to be used for performance assessment, or to significantly influence your courses or teaching. And don't be conned by the 'quality is free' myth – excessive time spent on evaluation to improve teaching, at the expense of your research, will cost you dearly in performance-related pay and promotion.

Gathering the information

There are two aspects to evaluation – the gathering of the information and the use of it in improving and developing the course and teaching. There are obvious simple performance indicators such as drop-out or failure rates, which are readily available, while evidence on teaching may be obtained from the students, you, colleagues and education experts. This may then be put to use by analysing the results, identifying weaknesses and taking action to correct these. Note that no single source of information should be regarded as definitive – construct your overall evaluation from a number of different sources, cross-checking the conclusions for consistency. This process of cross-checking is called *triangulation*.

Evaluation by students

Your students are experts in being taught. They have seen a lot of teachers, a lot of you, and given the opportunity will be only too happy to acquaint you with your deficiencies. There are three crucial things to remember about evidence from students however:

- Students can only make informed comment on a certain subset of your teaching activities – that is, only certain parts of Figure 1.
- Students' opinions on their teaching can only be subjective (but important none the less).
- Information on the students' learning process and its outcomes are as important as their views on the teaching given.

What can students tell you?

Before gathering evidence from students, you must have a clear idea of what information you require, since that will influence the method by which you seek it. You will certainly not be trying to get an objective view of the quality of the course and the teaching from the students – they are simply not qualified to make such judgements. The information you can obtain from them will be an indirect but invaluable input to the overall evaluation of the teaching. The main types of evidence you can obtain from students and their education are (Ramsden and Dodds, 1989):

- – Data on outcomes and processes of student learning.
- – Information on students' approach to studying.

- Students' perceptions of the course and teaching.
- Students' appreciation of course objectives.
- Students' opinions on the course and teaching.

Collecting student evidence

There are a range of methods of gathering the sort of information described above:

- Coursework and examination results.
- Inspection of students' work (including their notes).
- Interviews with students.
- Class discussion.
- Questionnaires.

You will see that any of these methods requires time and possibly other expenditure, such as secretarial or administrative assistance for questionnaires. Some also involve the students, taking up precious contact time.

Coursework and examination results

Coursework, examination results, other assessment statistics and performance indicators can often be obtained fairly easily. You will have your own record of those relating directly to your course and others, such as entry qualifications, should also be close at hand, if not part of your course documentation. Do not give them undue credence simply because they may come in a quantitative form – like publication and citation rates in research assessment, their validity and usefulness is not enhanced by attaching a number to them.

Students' work

Close inspection of students' work is essential if you want to know what assessment results really mean. You can start with a small sample of scripts to get a starting point for a more detailed search. You are not just looking for 'howlers', but for really fundamental misunderstandings and errors, which occur repeatedly, from a number of students. Also, from the general style of the work you can often detect what sort of learning approach they are using – for example, short, bitty answers, continually pulling out the easy parts of questions, may indicate a surface approach. Having compiled a list of common errors and misconceptions, then you can study these, identify their source, formulate remedies and cross-check with other components of the evaluation. Reading students' notes is often embarrassingly revealing, not to say hilarious. Again, it is the commonly occurring error or misunderstanding you are looking for. Also, the general state of the notes can indicate whether your pace is right, or your board skills are up to scratch. It may help if you obtain second opinions from colleagues, or other experts.

Interviewing students for evaluation purposes

Interviewing students can provide much information across the whole range of types, but it needs to be organized carefully. A general, aimless chat is futile – but no more so than a strict, formal interrogation. Decide on a number of specific issues that you wish to discuss, but do not tie yourself and the students down to precise questions. The sorts of things you might raise include not only specific course topics, related directly to the subject matter, but also more general points such as 'likes and dislikes', views on the teaching and assessment methods, understanding of course objectives, opinions of workload and suggestions for improvement. You will get the best out of the interview if you can encourage students to speak freely, make them understand that they are also assisting you in your evaluation and that you value their input.

We cannot all be experts at interviewing (as well as everything else) but a few simple rules are helpful – clarify vague comments by asking for more information or for a specific example; try to get students to rank their concerns in order of seriousness; elicit best and worst points about the course or teaching; check your understanding of their points by repeating them in your own words and confirming your interpretation with the students; solicit improvements on aspects criticized by the students (Ramsden and Dodds, 1989; Gibbs et al., 1989). It is rarely practical to interview all students and it is perhaps best to use interviewing to gain a rough insight into the major issues of concern before launching into other methods such as questionnaires. Also, of course, you may have the opportunity to get students' views from their representatives on staff-student committees – if you can rely on them to be truly representative.

Class discussion for evaluation purposes

Class discussion can be treated as an extended interview, but needs to be carefully structured to avoid degeneration into a hodge-podge of gripes. Gibbs et al. (1989) give a very effective method for doing this. Students, after time for reflection, are each asked to note a single good and a single bad point about the course, the teaching and the students. They then work in small groups to come to an agreed list of such points, containing only majority views. Each such point is then discussed by the whole class, in each of the six categories in the matrix (good course/bad course, etc.), again retaining only majority views. Further discussion, as time permits, may serve to clarify and enlarge on these issues which, finally, the teacher considers outside class in the light of other evidence, reporting his/her response to the students at a future meeting. Remember that such activities eat up contact time, however, and therefore may be impractical.

Questionnaires

Questionnaires are the most under/over rated, used/misused means of gathering student evidence there is. Quite simply, they are not a game for amateurs – which I am afraid is what most of us are in this respect. However, so long as you remember their limitations, apply them only in valid situations and treat them as simply one part of the evaluation, cross-checking them with other components, then you may be able to adapt one of the many now available in the literature, or even construct one yourself. Either Gibbs *et al.* (1989) or Ramsden and Dodds (1989) – also see Partington (1993) for a comprehensive batch of feedback questionnaires – will serve as a good practical guide for your choice of questionnaires, at least in your early attempts to obtain student feedback.

Rather than give an example of a questionnaire here – you have probably seen examples already – I will simply alert you to their complexities by describing some of the many kinds already available. The most basic questionnaires are usually aimed at finding out the students' views of the course and your teaching. If your department is paying lip-service to evaluation with some pirated questionnaire of a general nature, then it probably consists of half-a-dozen questions asking the students what they think of your knowledge of the subject, your ability to put it across, your organization and preparation of the course, your feedback to students and your concern for them. Such a questionnaire gives a broad picture of what is going on and may detect any major discontent among the students, but it doesn't really get you to the root of detailed problems. For this you will need a more sophisticated approach such as *progessive focusing*, described in Gibbs *et al.* (1989). This uses a system of diagnostic questionnaires, successively homing in on problems.

As well as seeking students' opinions of the course and your teaching, you may also need to look at *them*, to find out what effect your teaching is having on *their* behaviour. For example, you can use a *study questionnaire* to investigate the approaches to learning used by the students – if you uncover a widespread surface approach then you may need to change your teaching or assessment methods. Similarly, a *course perceptions questionnaire* will tell you whether the students see the course in the way you would wish. The students may have strong views on the content and objectives of the course, which conflict with your own. On using a *course contents* or *course objectives questionnaire* to uncover such differences you can decide whether to change your content or objectives, or to put more effort into explaining them to the students (the usual student gripe here concerns the 'relevance' of your course content – which rarely matches up to their expectations). Examples of all these questionnaires may be found in Gibbs *et al.* (1989).

Other types of questionnaires include comparisons between courses, or between the different teaching components of a course; detailed examination of the individual teaching activities in Figure 1 – planning and preparation, courseware, delivery, assessment; questionnaires on different teaching methods – lecture, tutorial, practical, open learning, etc. You name it, someone has produced a questionnaire on it.

I can hear you asking 'where am I going to find the time for all this?' You won't. This is why some departments simply jump through the teaching quality assessment hoops and circulate the first questionnaire which comes to hand, making a mockery of the evaluation process. Certainly aim for an efficient feedback mechanism, but be selective in your use of questionnaires, looking for the best quality evidence on the aspects and problems of greatest interest to you. Gibbs *et al.* (1989) remind us that rapid, efficient feedback on students' views can be obtained by 'instant questionnaires', completed in a few moments during class time. These can target very specific issues, but are usually a little rough and ready. It brings us back to the plain fact that good evaluation does not come cheap. One can, of course, use computers to produce (choosing from a *cafeteria* style database of questionnaire items) and administer (by terminal-based data collection) questionnaires; and to process the results. But this too is expensive – and, as Gibbs *et al.* caution us, the technology involved does not in any way enhance the credibility of the output.

A question test-question

If constructing your own questionnaire, don't ask questions which the students are not qualified to answer. Restrict questions to the likely concerns of the students. You can trawl for such questions by a few preliminary interviews or a class discussion, or an open-ended questionnaire asking simply for a list of good and bad points, or issues of concern. Do not ask a question unless you intend to act on the answer. Ramsden and Dodds (1989) recommend the following test for any question to be included in an evaluation questionnaire. What *action* would you take if:

- most students agree with it;
- most students disagree with it;
- most students are neutral about it;
- half agree and half disagree?

If you cannot decide a course of action for each response – drop the question.

How to question

Direct the questions at the respondent and don't ask them to surmise about the view of the class as a whole. Avoid vague, overstated or ambiguous items. Make clear the manner in which you expect response – either on a scale of say, 1 (agree) to 5 (disagree), or simply just agree, don't know, disagree. Don't introduce any implicit bias by revealing, either in question phraseology or in comments beforehand, your own views. Avoid seeking comparisons such as 'lecture/course A is better than lecture/course B'. Include some open-ended questions, such as 'what is the best feature of this course?', as these are often the most revealing. Aim for a 100 per cent response – less than 80 per cent is suspect. Also, for a small number of students (say fewer than 20) a questionnaire is perhaps less useful than classroom discussions or interviews.

Analysing the results

Analysing completed questionnaires is a skilled task and those targeted at a specific purpose will probably need expert interpretation as well as expert construction. As with the construction of questionnaires, their purpose will determine the degree of rigour required in analysis of responses. For a self-set questionnaire, for your own evaluation purposes, with proper regard to the vagaries of these things, it is probably sufficient to total the scores, prune the open-ended responses and use a relatively crude analysis. A more sophisticated, possibly professionally devised questionnaire may need careful and expert analysis if you are to derive the maximum information, with a measure of its reliability. In any event, numerical statistics obtained from questionnaires should not be imbued with any great quantitative significance, simply because they *are* numerical.

Question questionnaires

With the current emphasis on appraisal and performance assessment, student feedback questionnaires are becoming more widely used in universities. In view of the difficulty of constructing reliable questionnaires a word of warning is therefore necessary. If any questionnaire is used as a component in your appraisal or your performance assessment, insist on knowing its source, validity, reliability and objectivity, with the evidence to support these. Also insist on knowing the means of analysis and interpretation of the questionnaire responses, again with evidence to support the validity and reliability of these. Check on the respectability of the questionnaire and, if necessary, seek professional advice. If still in doubt consult your union or professional association. I have seen experienced teachers become very concerned over the use of student questionnaires and it is important that we all realize their limitations and susceptibility to misuse. Do not regard your head of department or any senior academic or administrative staff as experts in this field (they rarely have time to be) and do not allow them to use inappropriate, badly designed and invalid questionnaires. Treat a questionnaire exactly as you would any other academic or administrative document – with questioning, enlightened scepticism, and insist on evidence of provenance, validity and reliability.

Course Experience Questionnaire

A good, widely used feedback questionnaire, which has been thoroughly piloted and tested and which covers the whole range of teaching and learning experience can be found in Ramsden (1992) – the *Course Experience Questionnaire*. The questions (30 in all) are aimed at five categories – quality of teaching; clarity of objectives; appropriateness of workload; appropriateness of assessment and encouragement of independent learning. The questionnaire, aimed at the overall course experience, is not suitable for individual performance assessment or appraisal, but as an evaluative tool it is very useful. A word of caution, however. Some subjects, by their nature, are less suitable for independent learning than others (science and engineering less so than the arts and social sciences), and this may result in a less favourable CEQ score for these subjects.

Self-evaluation

Self-evaluation is probably the most important aspect of the evaluation process, providing it is done honestly, by a valid, reliable and objective process. Not only does it include careful, informed self-criticism of every aspect of the teaching activity, but it involves pulling together and corre-lating all the components of evaluation from the other sources – students, colleagues and educational experts. It also, nowadays, means thorough documentation of the evaluation process. It is time-consuming in the early stages and requires effort and commitment – but it is becoming part of the job. Schön (1983) has used the term *reflective practitioner* to refer to the way in which professionals monitor and enhance their performance by proactive self-examination. This is a nice characterization of the way in which good teachers are always thinking about their teaching, as they do it, analysing and evaluating it, and looking for improvements. Self-evaluation is the formalization of this.

Self-evaluation checklists

For your self-evaluation you can of course use all the methods of this chapter, depending on your resources. Again, you may use Figure 1, or your version of it, to provide a focus for your self-evaluation of different aspects of your teaching performance. For each activity you can, with the assistance of your students and colleagues, the literature and your staff development unit, devise a number of checklists defining some notion of good practice, against which you can compare your performance. If this is a little vague, it is because it depends so much on the subject, the context, your colleagues and many other factors. The important thing is to devise a self-evaluation strategy which suits you. Again, this seems like a lot of work, but once you have laid the foundations, the worst will be done and you will have a robust self-evaluation strategy for the rest of your teaching career. It will also form a good foundation for your teaching profile or other documentation required for performance assessment or appraisal. The following checklists for the different teaching activities in Figure 1 are merely offered as illustrative starting points to adapt to your individual needs. Your versions may look different, but if you have thought deeply and consulted widely then they will be right for you.

Planning and development checklist

- Are the course objectives well defined?
- Does the course commence at a point accessible to the students?
- Is the content and structure of the course consistent with its objectives?
- Is the course content appropriate to the required standard?

- Are the teaching methods planned appropriate to the course objectives and standard?
- Is there a range of teaching methods?
- Are the teaching methods adequately resourced?
- Is the proposed assessment method a valid and reliable measure of the achievement of the objectives?
- Is there a valid and reliable mechanism for student feedback and other evaluation of the teaching of the course?
- Is there a mechanism for responding to feedback and developing improvements in the course?

Courseware checklist

- Is the courseware adequately resourced?
- Are objectives and methods of assessment made clear to the students?
- Does it cover the objectives in a clear, structured, logical manner?
- Is it concise, accurate and balanced?
- Does it start from an appropriate point for the intended students?
- Is it pitched at an appropriate pace, level and standard?
- Is the amount of material appropriate to the duration and standard of the course?
- Is efficient and effective use made of prose, diagrams, layout and other presentational methods?
- Is the style appropriate and consistent?
- Does it provide students with sufficient activity to develop the required skills?
- Is it appropriate to the proposed teaching/learning activity?
- Is there a valid and reliable feedback mechanism by which to evaluate the courseware?
- How can the courseware be improved?

Teaching/learning activity checklist – the formal lecture

Checklists for the teaching/learning activity will depend on the teaching method adopted. If you use formal lecture methods you will find a whole industry based on providing evaluation of content, delivery and so on. A suitable checklist for monitoring your performance in a formal lecture might contain the following items.

- Did you display an expert knowledge of the subject?
- Did you introduce your topic in a clear, concise and interesting manner?
- Was the content appropriate to the time available and was it clear, interesting and developed in a logical and transparent manner?
- Did you emphasize the relevance of the topics?
- Was your voice right – clearly audible, enthusiastic – or monotonous, fading away at the end of sentences?
- Were difficult points treated clearly and comprehensively enough?

- Was your speed of delivery too fast, or too slow and did you use it to convey interest and emphasis?
- Was there enough variety in your presentation?
- Did you use board/OHP/other aids appropriately and skilfully?
- Did you use body language and gestures in a helpful way, to convey emphasis and energy?
- Did you have any distracting physical or verbal mannerisms?
- Did you maintain eye contact with the class?
- Did you keep students' interest and convey enthusiasm?
- Did you use audio-visual aids effectively, with well prepared material?
- Did you involve students in the class?
- Did you respond sensitively and helpfully to students' questions?
- Did you conclude your lecture with a concise summary of the key points covered, and a 'trailer' for the next lecture?
- Were students encouraged to see you outside class?
- Did your lecture maintain the continuity of the course?
- How could it be improved?

A checklist for active learning

In active learning the evaluation process also has to look at the extra dimension of your facilitation of the students' independent learning. You will need to add to your checklist items such as (CVCP/USDU, 1992):

- Do you develop personal autonomy and independence in students?
- Do you encourage and empower students to make their own decisions?
- Do you provide opportunity for the students to solve their own problems?
- Do students have freedom and support to manage their own actions?
- Do you encourage students to take individual and collective responsibility?

In fact, the good teacher will reply 'yes' to these questions whatever his/her teaching method. These questions are sometimes best answered by giving specific examples of the ways in which students are expected to decide the learning process for themselves, on your course (Habeshaw, 1989).

A checklist for small group teaching

Here we are looking at how well you facilitate the interaction within a group. You might ask:

- Was the group activity well planned and organized?
- Were the objectives of the session clear to all participants?
- Was the activity adequately resourced?
- Was the courseware appropriate?
- Did all participants make roughly equal contributions?
- Was advantage taken of mood, interests and topicality?
- Was independent activity encouraged?

- Did everyone have their particular problems addressed?
- Was the group kept on course towards the objectives?
- Did everyone consider the activity worthwhile?
- What were the bad points?
- How could it be improved?

An important question in small-group teaching is the extent to which you or the students controlled the session. A behavioural checklist asking 'Who is in control?', is described in CVCP/USDU (1992).

Open learning checklist

Even more so than in active learning, you will be looking here at the sort of facilitation and support you provide for independent activity. Thus, more emphasis needs to be placed on the quality of material you provide, the support you give, the sort of feedback and maintenance of progress which you provide, and on the effective use of the reduced opportunities for contact with students. A comprehensive checklist for open learning courseware may be found in Ellington and Race (1993). An overall checklist for effectiveness of open learning teaching is given by Rowntree (1990):

- Do learners have enough guidance on what is expected of them?
- Will learners have difficulty achieving any of the course objectives?
- How long would you expect learners to take over each section?
- Is the material pitched at the right level of difficulty and interest for the intended learners?
- Are the examples, analogies and case studies relevant to learners' interests and are they sufficiently illuminating?
- Can you suggest any additional examples, analogies and case studies?
- Are there any sections that are likely to cause problems for learners (or support staff)?
- Are all new terms adequately explained?
- Is the number and distribution of activities and/or self-tests about right?
- Are all the activities worthwhile and practicable?
- Does the assignment or suggested follow-up activity (if any) seem appropriate?
- Can you suggest any further ideas for activities, tests or assignments?

Student assessment checklist

There are three main aspects to consider when evaluating the assessment of students – the setting of the assessment, the marking and the administration and reporting of assessment and results. A checklist might include such items as:

- Is assessment prepared and set in good time?
- Is the assessment monitored, moderated or otherwise regulated?
- Are the students fully informed (in writing) of the method and timetable of assessment?

- Does the assessment include full written instructions on the timing, conduct and materials to be used in the assessment?
- Are students aware of the examination regulations?
- Is the assessment linked to course objectives?
- Is the assessment of the right standard?
- Is it a valid test of achievement of the objectives?
- Is it reliable?
- Is it fair and objective?
- Is the assessment linked to a precise, reliable marking scheme?
- Is marking fair and reliable?
- Is marking monitored/externally moderated?
- Are regulations for reporting results clear and publicized?
- Are your results reported in good time?
- Are Examination Boards alerted to special circumstances affecting students?
- Do you attend Examination Boards?

Evaluation checklist

As if evaluation itself were not enough to do, we really ought to evaluate the evaluation process itself! Perhaps the most important aspect here is that you check that not only is the evaluation process accurate, valid and reliable, but that you actually take action on the results of evaluation. A suitable checklist might be as below:

- Does evaluation cover every aspect of the teaching activity?
- Is evaluation composed of a number of components – student, self, peer, expert?
- Are the evaluation methods used accurate?
- Are the evaluation methods valid and reliable?
- Are the results of evaluation conveyed to the students?
- What actions are taken on the results of the evaluation?
- Are confidentiality and privacy protected?
- What means are taken to ensure that action taken following evaluation results in improved teaching?

SWAIN and RAIN

SWAIN is a self-evaluation technique in which you systematically reflect on your Strengths, Weaknesses, Aspirations and Interests in order to identify your Needs. For your *strengths* you must decide whether to consolidate, capitalize, extend or expand them. You can either seek to overcome your *weaknesses* by remedial activities, or you can elect to avoid them in your work. Your *aspirations* may involve you in new tasks, which will involve the development of new knowledge, skills and attitudes. Your *interests* are also important, since working on these is easy and pleasurable for you. Your reflections on these four areas will lead you to conclusions about what you *need* in order to address the issues which arise in the process. You can then set a timetable for tackling these issues, by training or whatever. RAIN is a self-explanatory variation on SWAIN based on your Role, Aspirations, Inhibitors and Needs (CVCP/USDU, 1992).

Course log-book/diary

Another aid to your self-evaluation is to keep a *course log-book* (Ramsden and Dodds, 1989). This is essentially a diary of the course, containing such things as topics covered, student reactions, weak and strong points, evaluation processes and their results and the actions taken, students' work, students' and colleagues' comments, etc. Certainly this is yet one more job and may seem too formal for some people's tastes, but don't forget that it will fulfil other functions – such as forming the basis for appraisal, performance assessment or a CV, or providing material for your teaching portfolio.

Evaluation by colleagues

Your colleagues will usually be less interested in the processes of your teaching and more in the outcomes. Are your course objectives consistent with their requirements? Do the students come from you with the background they need? Are your standards about right? You learn from your colleagues in a wide variety of ways, from the friendly chat in the corridor to the bitter contests at departmental meetings and Examination Boards. Also, you can perhaps ask a respected colleague to sit in on your lectures, if you need some feedback on your performance.

Properly briefed, a helpful and committed colleague/peer can obviously pass useful comment on all your teaching activities (and will readily do so, although not always to your face). They can also act as an honest broker or critical friend, or simply as a sounding board for your self-evaluation. With planning and preparation they can help by commenting on your outline plans and your courseware, using checklists based on those you use for self-evaluation. Similarly, they can evaluate your assessment methods and marking. For this to be most helpful it needs to be quite formal and therefore may involve them in substantial work, so make it worth their while. For evaluation purposes, it is best to use colleagues who are not too close to you, and who do not have a vested interest in the outcome of the evaluation. Gibbs *et al.* (1989) give useful guidelines for giving and receiving feedback to and from colleagues. If you are giving feedback, let the recipient kick off, keep comments specific and to the point, be positive and negative in equal measure, concentrate on issues over which the recipient has control, and get a third opinion whenever possible. If you are on the receiving end, shut up and listen, don't take offence or try to defend yourself, seek clarification and evidence, take notes for later reference and think of ways you can improve, asking your colleague for suggestions. And, of course, always respect confidences.

Classroom observation

Probably the best way in which your colleagues can help is by observing your classroom activity. This should be done in a formal, well organized and structured manner (CVCP/USDU,1992). The purpose of the observation must be clear to all concerned and the observer will need precise instructions about when to arrive, where to sit, whether to participate and what sort of feedback you would like from her/him. You will need to explain the observer's presence to the students and to let her/him know whether or not the students may be spoken to about the teaching. The observer will need to know what her/his activity must be in the classroom – to observe course content, for example, or the teaching process? Specify exactly what you wish the observer to comment on (for example, board-work, class control, pace). If there is to be more than one class observation, provide an overall observation plan and explain how this fits into the total evaluation procedure.

The classroom observation may be followed up by structured debriefing. Explain how and when you want to conduct the debriefing; what documentation you would like about the observation; what particular points you would like covered and so on. Explain what will be done with the outcome of the process and what action you will take to use it to improve your teaching. Keep observers informed of the progress of your evaluation, thank them for their help and for any particular ways in which they had a positive impact on your teaching. Do not take their comments personally. Concentrate on the *process* not the *person*!

Micro-teaching

Micro-teaching is a refinement of live classroom observation in which attention is focussed on a particular aspect of delivery, such as the way in which you start a lecture, receive and respond to questions, involve students, facilitate their independent learning and so on. The particular issues addressed may have arisen from student or peer feedback, or simply from your own desire to perfect a particular skill. Depending on your resources, it may involve videoing short snippets of teaching, or role playing, or a succession of classroom observations. Basically, you just keep trying until you get it right, then move on to the next problem. You will probably need help from your staff development unit to get the best out of micro-teaching.

A dry run for the quality assessor's visit

Note that classroom visits prepared by external inspectors for performance assessment of your teaching are of a different nature from that discussed here. The inspectors will be *assessing* the teaching performance, rather than evaluating it for the purposes of feedback and improvement. Of course, they will be looking for similar things – but they will expect to see them, rather than assist you in accomplishing them. One would hope that after an evaluation or two by a colleague you will be functioning adequately to satisfy such inspections. In any case the external inspectors would normally discuss your teaching after the observation and give you the opportunity to comment on their assessment.

The new teacher

Classroom observation of the proper kind is particularly valuable for new and inexperienced teachers. A couple of sessions sitting in on a novice's lectures can transform their performance, quickly alerting them to such elementary but understandable problems as poor boardwork, voice projection, pace, etc. The observer not only observes the teacher in action, but also the reaction of the students and the interaction between teacher and student. If you can persuade an experienced lecturer to sit through a few of your classes and discuss your performance frankly, then you will benefit tremendously – also the exercise will create a useful and rewarding bond with the observer who, I am sure, will become a trusted source of advice for the future.

A classroom checklist

As with student questionnaires, the classroom observation game can become very sophisticated and assume a forbidding technicality, with ratings for every aspect of your activity – every syllable you utter, every twitch of your muscles. A checklist for the sort of things the observer might be looking at could be adapted from the self-evaluation checklist for teaching activity. A good comprehensive example, summarized below, was constructed by the TLA Centre, Edinburgh University (CVCP/USDU, 1992):

Venue
Are seating, lighting, heating, audio-visual aids, etc. adequate? If not, could the teacher have improved matters?
Context
Was this learning session set in the context of other sessions, the rest of the course, and the supporting materials?
Structure
Was the teaching material clearly structured and sequenced ? Were key points clearly signposted?
Level
Was the session pitched at a level the students could cope with? Was any provision made for those who experienced difficulties?
Clarity
Was the material clearly presented and readily understood by the students?
Use of examples
Were illustrations or examples related to students' knowledge and interests, and helpful to the students' appreciation of key points?

Handouts and other materials
Was appropriate use made of handouts or other study materials? If so, were these helpful to students in summarizing, amplifying or reinforcing the lecture material?
Audio-visual aids
Was appropriate and effective use made of audio/visual aids?
Audibility
Could the teacher be clearly heard by all students?
Pace and timing
Was the teaching material presented at an appropriate speed? Did the teacher keep to time?
Enthusiasm and interest
Did the teacher present the material in a lively and enthusiastic way? Was students' interest in the subject matter sustained or enhanced?
Interaction
Did the teacher facilitate interaction? For example, were there opportunities for questions or comments and for students' interests, concerns or experiences to be drawn upon?

Monitoring of marking

The British Open University monitors the marking of all its tutors on a regular basis, to ensure objectivity and consistency of marking from, literally, Lands End to John o'Groats (and beyond). I find this a very healthy policy. It does make you mark more carefully if you know that there is a possibility that someone will be checking your marking. The sort of things which the monitor comments on are common to any formative assessment marking, such as coursework. A checklist for such marking is given below.

- Were your comments on the script clear and helpful?
- Did you use the student's solution to raise teaching points?
- Did you explain why the student's approach was wrong?
- Did you refer the student to relevant parts of the courseware?
- Did you treat the student in a sympathetic way?
- Did you give the student the opportunity to discuss matters further, if appropriate?
- Were your recommendations for corrective action encouraging and realistic?
- Did you show precisely where marks were lost?
- Did you return scripts promptly? Did you give appropriate pro rata credit for a partially correct answer?
- Were all significant errors picked up?
- COULD THE STUDENT READ YOUR WRITING?

I emphasize the last point because recent surveys reveal that up to 50 per cent of students find tutors' coursework comments illegible – and I'm feeling uncomfortably self-conscious...

Evidence from educational experts – staff development

I doubt that there *are* many educational experts with accepted credentials in university teaching. And they will not come cheaply. So, at the moment, it is unlikely to be practicable to get direct advice on your own teaching from a professional educational expert – particularly in scientific and technical subjects. But of course, if you can, then that is one more useful component for your total evaluation. Ramsden and Dodds (1989) list the sorts of things on which such experts might usefully comment. These include the description of the course objectives; the appropriateness of the teaching methods and their relation to the objectives; the validity and reliability of the assessment methods and their relation to the objectives; the courseware; feedback to students; student workload; curriculum structure and student choice and general support given to students.

Your institution may have a staff development or educational development unit and this *should* (I know, it doesn't) provide a substantial service for evaluation of teaching. A good university staff development unit would provide literature resources, questionnaires, checklists, advice on the topics discussed in this chapter, and on teaching generally. It would be able to help in the administration and analysis of feedback procedures such as questionnaires. It would have a network of suitable mentors, critical friends, classroom observers, throughout the university. There would be a mechanism for identifying and disseminating good teaching practice; promoting and evaluating innovative methods and advising on different teaching methods. Dream on! I cannot see how a university that fails to resource these minimal staff development requirements can assure the quality of its teaching. For a nice story of the growth of a staff development unit see the article by Sandra Griffiths in Ellis (1993).

What staff development units absolutely should not do is become involved directly in appraisal or performance assessment of individuals – their role should be one of evaluation only, otherwise they will be treated with suspicion and deference by university teachers, who will simply not be inclined to go along to expose their weaknesses. This confusion of roles explains the rather muted interest in staff development in some institutions and countries.

Documentation and use of evaluation of teaching

Documentation – teaching portfolios/profiles

Well-documented evaluation of teaching, and effective remedial action on any problems unearthed will provide useful evidence for such things as appraisal and performance assessment. Also, many institutions are currently struggling with the question of how to measure, encourage and reward good teaching. How does the teacher provide evidence of their teaching prowess? The idea of a *teaching portfolio* or *profile* (the terminology does not seem standardized yet – *teaching dossier* is also used), in which the teacher describes and records his/her teaching activities, initiatives and innovations, seems to be a strong favourite for this. Evaluation will provide an important component of such a portfolio (Gibbs, 1989; CVCP/USDU, 1992). While a portfolio could be used for appraisal, promotion, job applications or support for grant applications, I think the primary reason portfolios will catch on among university teachers will simply be one of personal and professional satisfaction. We write courseware, we write books and articles – but when do we ever write about our teaching? Stop reading now and imagine that an educated layman walks in and asks you for a written description of your teaching activities and their effectiveness during the last couple of years – what have you got? Timetables, syllabuses, some coursework and examination results? Is that all your job amounts to? Of course not. But there are plenty of people in positions of power and influence who profess to believing that it is – and teachers make it easy for them, by taking for granted the vast expertise implicit in good teaching. By creating a teaching portfolio we remind *ourselves* of the complexity and importance of the job we do – and that is reason enough.

A teaching portfolio might contain:

– details of all courses you teach;
– your courseware and teaching methods;
– changes and innovation in your methods, content, etc.;
– results of student assessment;
– student details and how you use them;
– endorsements and testimonials on your teaching;
– pedagogical publications;
– teaching evaluation records;
– appraisal records;
– external examiners' reports;
– minutes of staff/students committee meetings;
– relevant course reviews.

Ideas for constructing a teaching portfolio or profile may be found in Gibbs (1989) and CVCP/USDU (1992). Gibbs suggests 32 categories of evidence which your profile might contain, divided into six groups. The groups consist of educational aims and objectives; teaching methods; assessment; outcomes of teaching; evaluation; and evidence of continued study of teaching and learning. As always, adapt to your own circumstances. There are however some sensible guidelines for putting the profile together efficiently and effectively. First, there is no need to produce, *ab initio*, a specially written document. If you make a habit of filing all your teaching documentation, then you can select relevant items from this for your profile, with *very* short and punchy commentary in summary and support. As someone with giant contempt for image and gloss it pains me to agree with Gibbs in saying that your portfolio must be smart and presentable – indeed, these days you will probably get far more brownie points for the design on your cover than the scholarship inside. That's show business.

Triangulation – then action

On completion and documentation of an evaluation exercise we will no doubt uncover a number of deficiencies in some aspects of our teaching. There is every reason to react positively to these – we all learn by our mistakes and it is nice to find things on which we can improve. The first step is to analyse the results of the evaluation to identify specific problems. Make sure that you triangulate these results with a number of other components of the evaluation. For example, if a student questionnaire suggests that your pace is too fast and a classroom observer has made similar comments, then it does seem likely that you are going too fast. Be wary of, and investigate further, glaring contradictions in the evaluation evidence. Once substantial problem areas have been confirmed by triangulation, then you must decide on some corrective action, perhaps in consultation with students, colleagues and staff development unit. This should be done immediately after evaluation. Finally this action must be implemented – and seen to be implemented, monitored and documented.

Three reasons for a little evaluation

I can imagine a number of my very busy colleagues being a little sceptical about all this evaluation and documentation. Most of us are continually evaluating our teaching without the extensive time-consuming paraphernalia discussed in this chapter. We talk to students and colleagues all the time, we know when something is going adrift and we sort it out quickly. We do not always have the time for the sort of formal processes discussed here. I have a lot of sympathy with this view. There is much strength to it and it will be a major obstacle to establishing an ethos of formal evaluation in universities and in the smooth implementation of appraisal and performance assessment. I would make three points to try to persuade my colleagues of the merits of taking a closer look at evaluation and its documentation.

First, there is no doubt that good, open communication with students and colleagues is worth any amount of formal evaluation and should always be the first priority of any good teacher. But we do not all achieve this state of nirvana with students and even when we do, there is no guarantee that our joint efforts will identify or agree on all the problem areas. Evaluation is not really about such elementary things as delivery pace, which are easily recognized and corrected. It is about substantial problems, such as lack of clarity of course objectives, examinations failing to test fundamental concepts and so on. Can we really put hand on heart and swear that we would pick all these things up in the normal course of events?

Second, formal assessment of teaching performance *will* (*has*) come. Documentary evidence of good practice will be required – and evaluation is an inseparable part of good teaching. I suspect that in a few years time it will be a normal professional expectation that teachers maintain a teaching portfolio and possibly course log-books. I'm not suggesting that there would be any element of compulsion in this (although for new staff, on highly tenuous short-term contracts, there would be no difficulty at all in enforcing such things), simply that, for example, it would be a natural assumption by appointment or promotion boards.

Finally, the best reason of all, formal evaluation, documented and acted upon is good for everyone – it improves teaching, makes student learning easier and more pleasurable and reduces tension between teachers and students. If it has received little attention in the past this is because teaching as a whole has always been a poor relation to research in universities and students have had little option but to tolerate this (although, in the UK the Students' Charter *may* change that). Also, it is a highly expensive and *unresourced* activity. How is it to be funded? I doubt that it will be – it certainly will not be if academic staff do not start demanding the resources by entering wholeheartedly into the process, insisting on the necessary time and support. Also, staff will need encouragement to undertake such activity, which can only mean some sort of reward mechanism for good teaching – moves in this direction are already being made, and recognition of good teaching is long overdue.

Getting started for the busy teacher

The fact remains that in many countries the evaluation and profiling of teaching is a new departure for many university staff. So, how do you ease yourself into it without finally cracking-up under the burden of one more job? This chapter, and the references cited, are full of ideas and suggestions, but then how do *you* make sense of it all and evolve your own strategy, starting from scratch, with not a lot of time? As this is such a personal thing, I hesitate to make suggestions here, but on balance I think you may like some ideas on getting started, to pick up or disregard as you please. So what follows is a suggested programme for developing your own evaluation and profiling methodology as painlessly as possible.

Be realistic – take your time

It will take most teachers two to three years to get effective evaluation and profiling under way – a year to plan and prepare your strategy and materials, and to review and document the previous few years' teaching as a base-line; a year to introduce and pilot initial evaluation exercises; and a year to analyse the gathered evidence, introduce and monitor improvements, update your portfolio, and review the overall strategy. So this is a long-term job. Don't be over-awed by the magnitude of the task. You can take your time, working through it steadily, absorbing it gradually into your other duties. And don't devote *much* time to it until you see clear evidence that your institution rewards such activities.

Get organized

The longest journey begins with the first step. Get all your teaching materials, documentation, records, etc. organized, using Figure 1 or any scheme that suits you. I do think that a systematic organization scheme, whatever it is, *is* essential. Devising this may take longer than you expect (doesn't it always?) – maybe a few weeks – because a lot of reflection and trial and error may be needed before you get the system which is right for you. And it is probably best to get it right at the outset because chopping and changing later on can be surprisingly messy – even on a word processor! (Which folder does this document go in? Do I need multiple copies of this? You know the sort of thing.)

Start a retrospective teaching profile

Assemble a teaching profile for the previous two or three years, using your records and course documentation. Going back a couple of years helps you to establish a system and format and also may reveal patterns and problems in your teaching, which could provide useful subjects for evaluation exercises. First, you may need to do some reading on putting together a portfolio (see Bibliography), bounce ideas off your colleagues, or consult your staff development unit. Then you will probably make a lot of mistakes and false starts. But a few months of steady work should reward you with a tolerable first draft. At the same time, you can start reading and thinking about your evaluation strategy. Even though you may not have been involved in formal evaluation of your teaching in previous years, you can still include your informal self-evaluation and course development in your embryonic portfolio. This might also be a good time to do a SWAIN, or similar self-analysis, if you find it helpful.

Aim for a simple evaluation – next year

When you feel comfortable and prepared, start some simple evaluation exercises. If the timing is right for you it is probably best to start these at the beginning of the academic year, and it is preferable to delay, rather than rush implementation. Better to concentrate your efforts on one course instead of trying to cover all your teaching assignments in the first year. Start a course log-book. Keep your first evaluation exercises simple, but try to include a number of components – performance indicators, self evaluation, student feedback and peer evaluation. Performance indicators will consist of such things as students' qualifications and assessment statistics from previous courses, coursework and examination results, etc. For your self-evaluation you could use some simple general checklists, or some targeted at particular areas which concern you but which don't take up too much time. For student feedback, look for a good general questionnaire and, if you feel up to it, one directed at a specific issue. Other methods of obtaining student feedback can be left to future years – one step at a time! For peer evaluation, find yourself a handy 'critical friend' (not too critical and not too friendly) and observe samples of each other's teaching, check out each other's courseware, etc. This first evaluation could take you up to a year to plan and prepare. That's OK. It's important to get it right. All this preparation and subsequent implementation goes into your log-book and will be summarized in your portfolio. By the way – don't think that all this will be a drudge. If you have got this far in the book then you are clearly *very* dedicated to your teaching. So I guarantee that you will *enjoy* doing your evaluation and writing about your teaching in your portfolio. In fact, you will probably have to be careful not to become too absorbed in it.

Take stock and move on

After the first year of evaluation, analyse the results, learn the lessons and use them to devise improvements to your teaching. Briefly summarize in your teaching profile, and begin to think about your aims for the next year. Top of the list will be the implementation and monitoring of your improvements. Then you can start to experiment with a wider range of evaluation tools, other courses, new problems, etc. But don't overload yourself – or the students. You have been thinking and writing about your teaching, in some depth, for a year or two by now. (I'm not suggesting you haven't always done so, of course!) Survey what you have done and look for any publishable ideas which you can develop – now you are really on your way. Your portfolio should now be looking quite respectable and, at last, you have hard evidence of your teaching activities to lay before your appraiser, promotion board or whatever.

Chapter Seven

Improving Efficiency while Maintaining Quality and Standards

The need for increased efficiency

More students, fewer resources

No university teacher in the UK can fail to notice the dramatic increase in student numbers, coupled with reduction in resources, in recent years. This trend to a mass higher education system brings the UK ever closer to many European countries, America and Australia. So why should the UK be different? Why are British academics beefing about 'large' classes which many US teachers might regard as small-group teaching? Well, it is what you are used to. University teachers in the UK are not used to the high drop-out and failure rates common in many other countries with mass higher education systems. UK students are used to relatively easy access to their teachers and frequent opportunities to supplement formal lecture classes with small-group tutorials and one-to-one consultation (not that many avail themselves of the opportunity). No doubt, given time, UK academics and students could get used to the higher student-staff ratios towards which we are currently hurtling, even though few of us believe this is either good for the system or the country. The real problem is that we are not given time. Instead, we are burdened with additional administration associated with accountability, demands for higher research output, and the problems arising from wider access. We are expected to change rapidly to a lower quality system, with an accountability structure which penalizes lower quality. In fact the pressures for increased efficiency are no less severe in countries already into mass higher education – and they have already used up most options for accommodating cuts in resources.

Increased efficiency does *lower quality and standards*

This chapter is about institutional and individual methods of improving efficiency, without lowering quality or standards *too much*. I emphasize 'too much' because frankly I don't believe you can increase efficiency in university (or any other) teaching significantly without lowering quality, standards, or both. More students with, at best, static resources simply means that each student receives less attention from teachers and this means lower-quality education. Large classes mean *bad* education. Lower staff-student ratios mean, other things being equal, less interpersonal interaction and less knowledge of individual students and *how to get the best out of them*. Every teacher at the chalk-face knows that without the need for inconclusive statistical surveys. The same people who would cram our best brains into bulging classrooms would not countenance anything less than individual coaching for our best footballers and cricketers – so they know it too.

Efficiency at the expense of quality must be resisted

I don't believe we work so inefficiently, or are so lazy, or care so little for our students that there is significant slack in the system to be taken up by reduced resources. All we can do is try to hold the line on quality and standards until we feel that enough is enough (many of us are there already), at which point we protest, resist, and most important, we ensure that the students and the public understand that it is government under-funding which is responsible for lower quality and standards, not us. As academics we are by nature individualistic, and our cooperative and collegial activities are usually limited to service to the students and institution. Consequently, when the efficiency of our working practices is questioned we are often caught isolated and uninformed (the same might be said of accountability issues) – there is not the framework for united response that exists in our academic functions. So, as well as offering pointers to set you thinking, one purpose of this chapter is to raise the profile of this issue and provide a launch-pad for debate coming from within the academic profession, rather than outside. University teachers must lead the way where greater efficiency can reasonably be achieved, and be forewarned and armed when it cannot. By the way, while few of us would sacrifice quality of teaching or research to efficiency, look carefully at your *administrative* workload. Some of it is essential – that which increases efficiency and effectiveness, such as good timetabling, examination administration, admissions, delegation of duties, etc. Most of the rest can go if you need to lighten your workload.

Standards can be reduced in line with resources

You get what you pay for – sometimes. If resources for teaching are reduced, then a valid response is to reduce the *standard* of educational outcome while maintaining the *quality* of the educational process. Suppose, for example, large class sizes result from reduced resources. One can still provide good quality teaching – *but more slowly*. Simply reduce the course objectives to give you a content which is manageable in the less favourable teaching environment with which you must contend. In this way, the country gets what it pays for, while you still provide a good education for the students *within your resources*. In fact it may sometimes be possible to lower standards appreciably without noticeable effect – particularly in those subjects which are not required by subsequent teachers. Even in examinations monitored by external examiners it is difficult for them to know how much one teaches to the examination standard, or to relate courses from one institution to another. Also, if standards drop across the whole system then relative changes will be undetectable. Finally, of course, it may be *desirable* to lower standards if they fall in schools. In short, even if reliable measurement of standards is possible, there is little guarantee that their decline will be detected, or mourned.

Efficiency in teaching

Increasing efficiency in teaching, so far as teachers are concerned, means coping with lower staff-student ratios without additional effective work-load. More directly, the lower income per student must be used more efficiently to deliver the highest possible quality of education. There is little point in saying much about complicated measures of efficiency in teaching beyond the crude statement that, institutionally and individually, there is a need to teach more students with less time and fewer resources. One then looks for greater efficiency in all teaching organization and activities, at every level. This comes down to how you use your resources and how you do your job.

Resources

The cost of resources for teaching depends on the subject and on the teaching and assessment methods used. Theoretical subjects such as mathematics rely mainly on academic staff time, with little need for equipment or dedicated accommodation, while experimental subjects such as electrical engineering require significant resourcing for equipment and laboratory space. Such differences are reflected in the income per student – engineering students bring in much more than mathematics students. In efficient deployment of resources, the full implications of different teaching methods must be taken into account. For example, if CAL is used to increase teaching efficiency by savings in teacher contact time, then the additional resourcing needed for support staff, hardware, maintenance, accommodation and training must be set against such savings. Further, the use of certain resources has implications for quality. For example, post-graduate demonstrators and part-time teachers are a relatively cheap teaching resource, but they inevitably lower the quality of service when compared with permanently available, fully qualified academic staff.

Estimating time and resources

Figure 1 again

Figure 1 provides a useful framework for consideration of efficiency gains in teaching a given course. Using Figure 1 we can itemize the cost of giving a course, by a particular teaching method, either in terms of staff/student time or in terms of resources such as equipment and accommodation. This can then be used to compare a number of different teaching strategies, for the same course objectives. For example, Figure 4 (see page 134) shows the cost in time and resources for preparation and delivery of a fictitious course forming $\frac{1}{36}$ of an honours degree programme by the formal lecture method, supported by tutorials, assessed by coursework and three-hour examination, over a typical lifetime of say, five years. Figure 5 (see page 135) shows the cost of running the same course over the same period using open learning with lecture time halved and 40 per cent continuous assessment, with a two-hour examination. Of course, the data used is very subjective and not to be taken seriously. The examples give only a crude comparison – and some things, such as preparation time, are difficult to estimate. However, 'costing' your teaching in this way, comparing strategies and estimating 'savings', does crystallize interesting teaching questions, and also helps you to manage your time and resources. Unless substantial benefits can be demonstrated as a result of such comparisons, you are better off sticking with your preferred teaching method, and tinkering with that, than moving to a 'more efficient' method – particularly if the students share your preference.

The examples of Figures 4 and 5 illustrate the main problems in comparing teaching strategies. Alternative strategies must all be capable of achieving the required course objectives. The facilities and resources required for each strategy need to be identified and costed. The time required for each component activity must be estimated. Unless you are going in for something very hardware-intensive, like computer-assisted learning, then the biggest problem is likely to be in allocating the teacher's time. This is very difficult to quantify, depending on the course, the teaching method, your state of prior preparation, your commitment to teaching, the expectations of the institution and of the students and your facilities and resources. The major time requirement relates to preparation, contact and assessment.

Load models

There is a current fashion for 'load models' in some departments, seeking an equitable distribution of workload among staff by numerical accounting procedures, rather than by traditional informal cooperation. If such a load model can be arrived at by consensus, then it is probably unnecessary; if it rankles then it is a waste of time; if it is imposed then it has to be opposed. The problem with formal load models is that estimates of the time required for the different activities are so contentious that the time taken in reaching and maintaining agreement, and the damage done to the collegial fabric, far

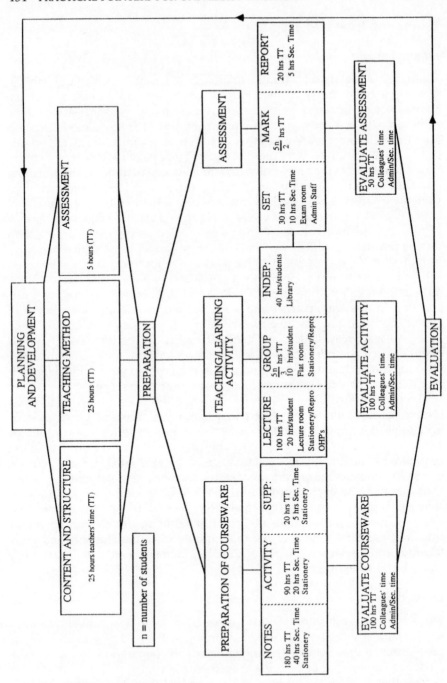

Figure 4   *The teaching activity: resource requirements of a course by formal lecture over five years*

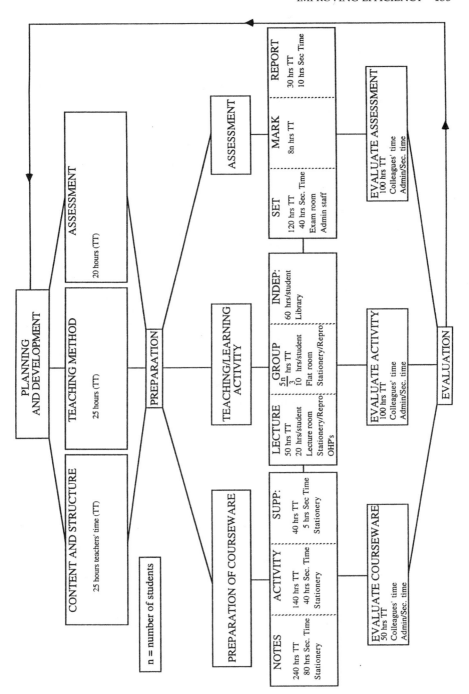

Figure 5 *The teaching activity: resource requirements of a course by open learning over five years*

outweigh any benefits over an informal approach. Informal arrangements are regarded as sloppy or lacking accountability by those who seek security in arithmetic balance sheets. However, the good academic leader uses a balance sheet of the commitment, expertise, aspirations and talents of his/ her staff and knows that the vast majority will do far more for their students and colleagues than their contractual obligations demand. This is not romanticism, but hard-headed nous about getting the best out of a bunch of people who will do more if they don't have to than if they do. I am happy to ask the questions a load model addresses, as in the examples of Figures 4 and 5, but I would never presume to answer them for anyone but myself, and I would never allow anyone to answer them for me.

Preparation time

For the experienced teacher the estimation of preparation time is not a big problem – he/she will have a fairly good idea from previous courses and will also know lots of short cuts if the preparation looks like getting out of hand. However, even an experienced teacher may have less idea of the extra preparation time required in a significant change of teaching method, say from formal lecture to open learning or use of computer-assisted learning. As noted elsewhere the novice teacher usually underestimates preparation time and needs experienced guidance on this point.

Not all preparation time is of equal weight. Some aspects of preparation, such as writing the core notes on a conceptually difficult topic, require deep concentration and thought and may require a solid 2 to 3 hour session without disturbance – prime time. Other aspects, such as constructing problem banks or checking mathematical proofs, are relatively routine and can be relegated to boring committee time or intermittent TV watching time.

Contact, assessment and evaluation time

Contact time is easily quantified from your timetable, but do not forget the *ad hoc* student consultation time, which may be substantial for a large course. There is an important difference between preparation and contact time. Preparation time is at your disposal, whereas contact time is relatively inflexible, controlled by someone else. So, the less contact time, the better you can manage your time, which is one good reason for considering open learning methods. Assessment time comprises setting, invigilating, marking and attendance at boards. Only setting is really at your disposal. The time spent on evaluation and development of your teaching and courses is largely up to you, but in these quality-conscious days you are entitled to insist on a reasonable amount.

Cost of resources

Figure 1 can also be used to compare the resource costs of different teaching strategies. In most cases this will actually be a minor consideration compared to staff time. Thus, for example, use of print-based open learning material certainly requires more paper, copying facilities, secretarial time and other support than does the formal lecturing approach – but it is doubtful whether the additional cost is large compared to staff costs. And of course it not only brings savings in staff time, but also in accommodation costs and flexibility of timetabling. However, if one used a computer-based open learning approach, then one must count the cost of the computing facilities, their maintenance and replacement and associated support staff.

National and institutional efficiency initiatives

Efficiency gains at all levels

Efficiency gains may be sought at different levels and by different stake-holders. Government departments will look for efficiency gains on a national scale. This may include encouraging and funding such things as franchising between institutions; national curricula; information technology infrastructure; changes in the conditions of service of teaching staff to include appraisal, performance related pay, etc. The role of national institutions such as the Open University in Britain might be expanded, or teaching-only universities might be established. At the institutional level, universities may look for more efficient course and programme structures, possibly through modularization. They may look at different teaching methods, or the use of information technology and computer-assisted learning. They will certainly look for increased student recruitment at the lowest possible cost. Greater use might be made of part-time and post-graduate personnel. At the level of the individual teacher, which is our primary interest here, we would be looking at more efficient teaching and assessment methods, improved personal organization and administration, increased lecture loads and larger classes.

National and institutional measures

Before considering ways of increasing efficiency at the individual level it is worth looking at the sorts of national (even global) and institutional measures which may affect you. Some you may embrace enthusiastically, others may have less appeal and you may need to be forearmed to deal with them. In terms of your teaching function, the most likely implications for you will be of the following types:

- Increasing teaching load for some staff;
- Increasing class sizes on courses given;
- 'Modularization' by combining classes in the same or closely related subjects;
- Changes in course and programme structure;
- Use of more efficient teaching methods;

- Increased use of part-time staff;
- Increased use of information technology and computer-assisted learning.

Increasing teaching load for some staff

Without reduction in administrative or research workload, this is essentially a demand for greater productivity without extra pay and is likely to be resisted. However, provided conditions of service and contractual obligations of academic staff are appropriately redefined, it is possible that significant numbers of staff may be pleased to increase their teaching load, if relieved of the obligation to do research – particularly if teaching enjoyed a similar career structure to research in higher education. But most departments have probably already strenuously explored such options – differential lecture loads have long been standard practice in most institutions – on a voluntary and collegial basis. I think the possibilities of persuading academic staff to spend more time teaching are therefore strictly limited. Even if staff can be persuaded to take on significant extra teaching duties, this may not be in the best interests of the students, or consistent with good quality teaching.

If you are asked to take on extra teaching, and you feel that the request is unreasonable, then consider your position carefully before responding. In the past such things have often been sorted out amicably in corridor or coffee-room discussions. There has always been the occasional awkward cuss creating problems, but that is the price you pay for getting 150 per cent out of the rest. Now, with new (and often short-term) contracts for some university teachers, and new disciplinary procedures for most, a more formal approach may be called for. If, on careful consideration of your contractual obligations and taking appropriate advice, you still feel that the request is unreasonable, then make your refusal in strictly formal terms by whatever official procedure is in place. Do not volunteer information which is not requested, and do not fall for the 'you have to do what your head of department tells you' line – which omits the matter of reasonableness, on which your head of department will not be the final arbiter. Force the system to deal with your case meticulously. That alone will probably take you past the starting point of the course under contention, through no fault of your own – not forgetting your need for preparation time! Always retain the moral high ground (but with a cold eye on the real terrain), with your refusal based on lack of resources, or excessive workload which would undermine the quality which the students and funding bodies are entitled to expect. At the end of the day, if your institution insists, work strictly to contract – they will get far less out of you than if an amicable solution had been arrived at. It pains me that I feel the need to broach such matters in a book on teaching, but I'm afraid that this is the reality for some teachers these days. See Habeshaw et al., (1992) for other suggestions for defending your position in these uncivilized times.

Increased class sizes

This is perhaps a more feasible means of improving efficiency and may be achieved either by increasing recruitment to degree programmes, or by modularization – combining groups of students on different degree programmes. But there are limits to recruitment because of the size of the qualified student pool, and lecture room accommodation will limit the size of classes. In fact, many institutions have long ago fully modularized in principle, if not in name. Indeed, there is growing feeling, at least in Britain, that things have gone too far in this direction and departments are increasingly requesting more bespoke material for their subject and requiring a more dedicated approach for their students. In any event, as mentioned earlier, larger classes mean lower quality education.

Reduce student contact time on a given course

If we do not reduce standards by lowering the course content then this effectively amounts to requiring students to teach themselves certain portions of the course material. For example, a teacher may halve his number of lectures and give the students directed reading or self-learning material for the routine subject content, reserving his lecturing for difficult aspects of the course. If we assume that students come to university to enjoy maximum contact with experts in their subject, then obviously such an approach is a real lowering of the quality of their education. Despite criticism of the lecture method, few practising teachers would deny that two hours of lectures is at least twice as good as one. Furthermore, why should students pay fees and burden themselves with loans for the privilege of teaching themselves?

However, provided well-prepared dedicated courseware is used and support facilities are first rate, the students may welcome the independence and flexibility offered by such teaching. They would receive training in self-learning techniques, self-help groups, etc., and rapid feedback could be arranged by computerized marking of regular tests. The initial preparation of material would have a financial cost as well as placing a heavy additional burden on academic staff, but if substantial reductions in teaching time could be achieved, then that price might be worth paying. Such schemes have already become popular in the USA (the Keller plan or personalized instruction – Bligh *et al.*, 1981; Keller and Sherman, 1974), mainly for their *effectiveness* rather than as a means of increasing efficiency in teaching. Significantly, however, they have failed to take off in the UK. This may be because their introduction in the early 1980s coincided with the cuts in university funding, and staff and institutions had neither the time nor resources for the highly intensive initial preparation required. Of course, this would be even more true today. However, funding bodies could overcome the problem by targeting dedicated pump-priming funds at the development of such resource-based learning (the Higher Education Funding Council for England has already begun a programme of funding pilot projects encouraging flexibility in course provision, which does exactly this).

Part-time staff, postgraduates and teaching assistants

Obviously, postgraduate demonstrators and qualified part-time staff are much cheaper than permanent academic staff. However, making use of them has its limits and, in fact, such casualization of the university teaching profession has probably gone as far as is reasonable, and much further in some cases. Postgraduates are rarely suitable for more than tutorial assistance – and why should they expose themselves to the very severe stresses of mainstream teaching for the meagre remuneration they receive? Part-time teachers, with the best will in the world, have lower commitment to the institution and possibly the students. They are less available for consultation, often cannot sit on Examination Boards and have limited institutional standing. Their employment conditions are often too insecure to allow them much independence or protection in disputes with students or other teaching staff. Also, of course, they do not contribute to such things as research ratings. It is possible that conventional universities could make greater use of part-time staff, but more careful consideration needs to be given to their precise duties, contractual obligations and conditions of service than is usual at present. The British Open University provides a useful model here. It contracts part-time tutors for very specific teaching and assessment duties, under controlled and monitored conditions. The conventional universities could operate similar schemes and may have the added advantage of being able to offer attractions such as accommodation, use of equipment and library resources, etc. In the USA there is widespread use of paid undergraduate and graduate teaching assistants, particularly in large classes (McGee, 1991). This provides relatively cheap support for some delegated teaching functions and useful income, experience, and training in teaching for the assistants. Such schemes are also taking off in the UK, if only to boost recruitment of postgraduate students by supplementing their income.

Information technology and computer-assisted learning

The use of these is the favourite hobby horse of non-teaching 'managers', administrators, government officials and civil servants who see it as the cure for all teaching ills. It is far less enthusiastically embraced by practising teachers simply because it is extremely expensive, highly labour intensive and its efficacy is totally unsupported by available testimony. There is no evidence that an hour in front of a computer screen has superior educational value to an hour in a lecture, or an hour spent reading a book and working through exercises. Indeed, there is growing evidence to the contrary. Also, there is no conclusive evidence for the cost effectiveness of computer-assisted learning over traditional teaching methods.

However, there are some very good teaching packages in some subjects, both for teaching core material and for *some* remedial work where the student dips in to particular topics needing some extra treatment. The best of these are interactive, allowing the student to switch readily from screen to pencil and paper. These tend to be better at the more routine information- or techniques-based teaching; they simply do not have the discursive facilities to explore and expand on deep conceptual topics requiring careful thought – a well-written textbook is far better for this and a good lecture or two even better. So, you may be able to use such packages for the routine stuff, concentrating a smaller number of lectures on the really difficult key topics.

CAL teaching packages are, of course, also limited by the accommodation and computing facilities available. The courseware must be compatible with a sufficiently wide range of equipment to provide a credible, accessible facility for the students who need it. Computing laboratories must be large enough and available enough. Information technology can also be useful in non-teaching functions, such as automatic marking of multiple choice tests, or for administrative and organizational purposes. Such applications can lead to real efficiency gains. Further ahead, but even more exciting, are the opportunities for the student which expert systems, networking facilities, and computer conferencing will provide for wider discourse in his own and related subjects (Laurillard, 1993).

Improving efficiency in your own teaching

Examine every aspect – Figure 1 yet again

This section looks at ways in which you may improve efficiency in your teaching activities. Anyone who has been teaching for the last few years will already be up to all these tricks, and more. That, or they have already been reduced to nervous wrecks. But there may still be some ideas you haven't thought of to lighten your burden. The rush of recent books on teaching large classes (Gibbs, 1992b; Gibbs and Jenkins, 1992; Habeshaw, *et al.* 1992; McGee, 1991) is no coincidence, and you can consult these for further ideas. The important thing is to examine closely every aspect of your teaching to remove wasted effort, find short cuts and identify priorities. We can again use Figure 1 as a basis for this. Breaking this down, the things we have to look at are:

- planning and development of courses;
- preparation of teaching material;
- presentation of lectures;

- small group teaching;
- student consultation;
- assessing students;
- evaluation of teaching.

Some general points

Before examining the component teaching activities, some general observations on coping with reduced resources and/or increased student numbers are worth noting. You can save yourself a lot of grief by good organization, planning and preparation. Essentially, you have more jobs to do for more people, and that means more opportunities for time-consuming errors, misunderstandings, queries and problems. Providing the students (and others involved in the teaching, such as teaching assistants) with clear and comprehensive information in the form of a course handbook will head off many of these. As well as course objectives, syllabus, book list, etc. this can also include such things as campus/departmental map, relevant staff with means of contact, student services and training facilities, calendar and important dates, assessment procedures, regulations, and deadlines (Habeshaw *et al.*, 1992).

Identify recurrent tasks, such as returning coursework comments, and get these as organized and automated as possible. Develop a systematic procedure for dealing efficiently with these tasks, making best use of paperwork, computers, support and administrative staff. Similarly, organize your course administration. This includes such things as your information gathering – availability of library resources, background of students (very difficult if your students come from a range of departments – make it easy for them to provide the information you need), and so on. Construct a set of standard letters, forms and spreadsheets, so that repetition is minimized.

Be realistic. Significant reduction in resources cannot but reduce the range of your activities. You may need to be more selective about the students you can afford special attention. Leave the best and the bulk to fend for themselves and concentrate on identified students, funnelling them into dedicated tutorials if you feel they can be helped. You may have to be more ruthless about those students, whom we have all met, that you know from day one are not going to make it, but you try anyway – perhaps you can redirect them at an earlier stage, to your mutual advantage. Another possibility is to reduce your course objectives – cover less material. I would bet that most courses you teach contain too much material for thorough treatment, in any case.

Help the students to help you. Many methods suggested for increasing efficiency of teaching require training the students in various transferable skills. The acceptance, as a basic educational principle, of this need to train students to manage their own learning, is liberating for both the students and yourself. Open learning, CAL, group- and peer-assessment, all come into this category. The general principle is the motivation behind the RSA initiative of Higher Education for Capability based at Leeds Metropolitan University and the University of Leeds (Stephenson and Weil, 1992). Such training may require changes in the curriculum and in teaching methods and assessment, and may imply foregoing some subject matter content. But the skills learnt are probably more educationally useful. Also, you will need to help students to combat the isolation and impersonality which they inevitably feel when plunged into the mass higher education system. This is essential for *your* benefit as well as theirs, because unhappy students learn badly, fail exams and therefore cause you problems.

McGee and friends – welcome to the asylum

The collection of essays on *Teaching the Mass Class* edited by Reece McGee

(1991) is a must for any university teacher – put in your inter-library loan request immediately. These people know what they are talking about. The sardonic humour, the deep thought about teaching, the wealth of practical hints, and the obvious pride and love for their calling make this a little gem. McGee defines the mass class as anything exceeding 250 students, but admits that the special problems such classes bring can arise with much smaller numbers. Essays include reports of harrowing experiences with large classes (not for the faint-hearted), use and training of teaching assistants, CAL in large classes, use of computers in course administration and organization, application of theatrical skills to large-scale lecturing, a survival kit, and much besides. The essayists, not always genteel, don't mince words and you're not shielded from the reality – I'm never sure McGee is joking when he says, 'If they are carrying weapons, it's time for the Dean'. Great stuff.

Problems with large classes

Some teaching activities are relatively independent of class size – lecturing to 100 students is little more arduous than lecturing to 40, for example. However, significantly larger classes *do* bring special problems – less interaction and lower feedback for example. Similarly, preparing the teaching material is largely independent of class size – except, of course, that whereas you may be able to justify full printed notes for 40 students, this may be prohibitive for 100 students and you may have to change your teaching methods. Larger classes will mean more tutorial groups. The time spent on consultation on student problems and on personal tutoring will increase significantly. Coursework and examination marking will, of course, increase but at least it is confined to a small part of the year. In the same way, examination invigilation just means a few more scripts to gather and Examination Boards may take a little longer. So we can cope with the problem of somewhat larger classes with not *too* much trouble from the point of view of lecturing – but of course, they present very considerable problems for other teaching methods such as group discussions, or laboratory work. *Very* large classes (the mass class – see below) create major problems, even for lecturing.

Problems with extra courses

More serious problems arise when the increased workload comes in the form of extra courses, that is, when there is a significant increase in your teaching hours. If the research funding to your department is reduced then the implication is that you should devote more of your time to teaching, rather than research. So, whereas say 12 hours a week may have been regarded as the norm in your department in the past, you may now find yourself required to do 14 hours a week or more. If this apparently innocuous increase comes in the form of two extra 30-hour courses per year then this is a significant increase in workload and you will be looking for substantial improvements in efficiency to make this tolerable, while at the same time maintaining the quality of the learning experience for the students. All your teaching activities increase proportionately, of course. Offsetting this may require significant changes in teaching method, contact time and assessment procedures, over and above those implied simply by large classes. The effect of your extra workload on the students and the quality of the teaching must also be considered.

Efficiency in planning and development

You can economize on course planning by using already available resources such as a set textbook or off-the-peg open learning or CAL packages (although these have other, possibly more time consuming, planning implications). You may have to compromise a little on your course objectives, but these are hard times in education and it may be that designing your own course from scratch is now a luxury you can't afford. Some methods of student assessment are easier to plan than others. A single sessional examination at the end of the course requires virtually no planning at all, whereas use of continuous assessment can require careful planning. When should it be set? On what topics? How much does it contribute to assessment? If you abandon continuous assessment altogether then you may be changing your course objectives and you will certainly be degrading your teaching method. You can economize on evaluation of teaching by simply not engaging in formal self-evaluation, but leave it to others to devise and administer student questionnaires and other feedback. That is, don't plan it at all.

Efficiency in preparation

Again, if you adopt a textbook, or other off-the-peg courseware then you can dramatically reduce your preparation time. Similarly, use of someone else's notes and problem sheets can save a lot of time. At a departmental level a centralized resource of teaching material for all courses in its programmes, particularly the basic, heavily used courses, should become the norm in future years – the experience, expertise and courseware of a teacher should not leave with him, leaving a newcomer to start all over again. Similarly, such a central resource allows greater flexibility by making it easier for staff to switch between courses. So, one way of saving preparation time is – don't prepare, use someone else's material. Some time will, of course, be needed in adapting it to your needs.

Course preparation is full of opportunities for displacement activity, time-wasting and general prevarication. If you let it, finding the perfect way to present a topic can take hours of anguishing over every last syllable. Draft after draft is trashed, and you can't stop tinkering with it. And invariably the first draft was perfectly adequate. The antidote to this is to be ruthless and set yourself rigid deadlines and targets – and stick to them. Be easily satisfied – as long as you can get something half sensible, leave it at that. You often find that on later rereading, or during the lecture, the right form just pops out (thank heavens for the unconscious). Pick your colleagues' brains, lift a passage out of a book, pare down to essentials, and if in doubt leave it out.

'Hard' and 'soft' preparation

Split your courseware preparation into 'hard' and 'soft' parts, the hard being the difficult, subtle and deep topics, the preparation of which requires careful thought, while the soft is the routine material which is easy to produce and cover. Allocate substantial chunks of undisturbed time to the hard parts and give priority to getting the associated material prepared first, irrespective of its place in the course sequence. You may need time to mull over this material, for the students' sake. On the other hand, the soft material you can afford to risk rushing and can slot into the odd free hour. This is just good time management.

Efficiency in lecturing

Here we are looking at lecturing less or lecturing to larger classes. We have already described open learning methods which allow you to transfer the responsibility for learning to the students, and to reduce your lecturing time (along the lines of the independence strategy of Gibbs, 1992b). Other possibilities include peer-tutoring and computer assisted learning. In such methods, you may still be giving lectures, but they will be of a different kind, providing overview, motivation, targeting difficult areas and so on. But, so far as lecturing is concerned, the real increase in efficiency comes from larger classes. A great deal of work has been done on this in recent years, and we can only scratch the surface here (see Bibliography).

Lecturing to large classes

Everything said about 'normal' teaching applies for large classes, but more so. Your resources must be more than adequate, and deliverable on time; your planning has got to be military; your preparation meticulous and *well in advance*; accommodation and equipment must be up to the job; teaching, clerical and administrative assistants must be well briefed; and your delivery has got to 'enlarge' to reach the back row. You simply cannot afford hitches in the large class. Just getting them all in and seated, or distributing materials, takes precious minutes off contact time. Minor disruptions multiply. The problem of heterogeneous background and abilities magnify. Problem students become sizeable groups. The black/white board becomes inadequate and even OHP projection may have its limitations for the mass class.

Analogy with theatrical performance provides useful guidelines for lecturing to large classes (McGee, 1991). Think of your class as an audience. Theatres (and audiences) do not welcome latecomers once the performance has started. Strict silence is observed, and the performers demand, and must hold, the attention of the audience. The performer's diction and voice projection must be good and variations in pitch, volume and intensity must enliven the script. Body language and gestures need to be larger and more purposeful. Play to everyone, including the back row. Move about the stage, and among the audience, to reduce interpersonal distances. Exude enthusiasm. Know your lines and rehearse delivery. Maintain a brisk pace to hold interest. No one suggests that the whole lecture need be conducted as theatrical monologue; indeed, I have already referred to the exciting possibilities for active learning in large classes described by Jenkins (Gibbs and Jenkins, 1992). But when you do have to lecture, your first priority is to get your message across – so take a few lessons from the Thespians and the talk-show hosts.

Controlling the large class

Large classes need controlling with an iron fist – in a velvet glove. This is not because of unruly students – there are probably very few of these anyway. It is simply necessary in order to handle a large number of lively and boisterous individuals who can think of better places to be than your lecture. You *need* a disciplined environment, and they can *use* it. Some teachers frown on such authoritarian ideas, arguing that they can teach better in a more enlightened atmosphere. Perhaps they can. But the magic in their personality which enables them to do so is granted to few, and control is by far the best default option for most of us – particularly the novice lecturer. However, we are all slaves to our personality. You may simply be incapable of exercising control and commanding compliance in a large group of people. You may not even be able to play-act such behaviour. This is no shame on you, we cannot all be thick-skinned hard cases. But I'm afraid it does mean that mass class teaching is not for you. I think McGee and friends will convince you of that.

If you do decide to brave the large class your greatest assets will be self-confidence, organization and a sense of humour. Your greatest enemy will be the stone-cold fear you feel before and during the lecture (McGee is thoughtful enough to tell us that fear of speaking to groups is reported as most people's worst fear). For ways of combating this you cannot do better than consult McGee's survival kit. If you can't get a copy before your next large lecture, here are a few tips. Don't even try to be perfect – accept that you will make a fool of yourself sooner or later, and be prepared to laugh it off when you do. The students will think better of you for it. Have confidence in your knowledge of the material – or learn it until you have. Shrug off the paranoia – the psychotic thugs of your school days have long since matriculated to other institutions, and what you have before you is a fairly civilized slice of humanity who will be easy to handle and control if you are reasonable with them. Indeed, the knowledge that most students (and, dismally, academics) in fact *welcome* authority and direction, provided it is fair and responsive, is your best secret weapon.

The larger class does mean more student queries or challenges during the lecture, again using up precious minutes. Handling these is particularly crucial. Dismissing them out of hand can sour the atmosphere, adding to your difficulties. Exhaustive treatment of them all is impractical. Forbidding all student intervention during the lecture *is* an option, provided students are made aware of the reasons for this and have ample alternative means of quizzing you. Perhaps the best compromise is to explain your problem to the students and ask them to be sensible about interruptions – Kain, one of McGee's friends, suggests telling the students exactly how much money is wasted on non-productive disruptions! McGee's survival kit contains a number of tips for handling student challenges, which may get you out of trouble. Don't threaten a sanction you can't enforce; take all challenges seriously; explain your actions; seek class opinion; remain courteous and admit errors; react pleasantly and reasonably and don't let it get personal; don't back anyone into a corner; and, if all else fails, close the session, allow feelings to settle down and sort the problem out for the next session.

Maryellen Weimer, another of McGee's friends, gives a nice essay on classroom management, which echoes the experiences of many of us (McGee, 1991; see also Weimer, 1987). She addresses four crucial issues in teaching the large class: establishing yourself as a teaching force to be reckoned with, handling disruptions, encouraging a conducive learning environment, and getting student feedback. The rules of the game may be summarized in general terms. Give clear unambiguous messages, in written, verbal and action form, as to how the class will be conducted. Get to know as many students as reasonable, by name, by pressing the flesh, pleasantries, and so on. Possess the environment – be in the class before and after the students. Move about among the students, so that none of them feels safe! Establish control right from the start. Don't let small infractions pass, but use them gently and firmly as a means of reinforcing the rules of conduct. Avoid definite, inflexible, public statements on which you may later retreat. Be sure of your power and authority. Help the students to get to know each other, thereby enhancing the power of peer pressure. Ensure that the students know that education is not entertainment, and that learning is not always easy, or fun. Develop mechanisms for fast effective feedback on student progress, such as instant questionnaires, selective surveying, over coffee, etc.

Videoing lectures

I suppose the ultimate efficiency in presenting lectures is to have them videoed for future use, so that you never have to appear in person again. The videos may also be used anywhere, any time, as part of distance learning packages, for example. I am afraid I cannot enthuse about this, for two reasons – a videoed lecture is so far inferior to the actuality as to be virtually valueless, and I have yet to be convinced that it is not extremely expensive and inefficient. Some years ago we had very large groups of first year engineering mathematics students, for which large enough lecture rooms were simply not available. The 'solution' was to use closed circuit television with the teacher in one 'active' (now there is an interesting twist on active learning) room and closed-circuit television in two other 'passive' rooms. At the start of every lecture there was a mad rush to get into the active room and the overflow students, banished to the passive rooms were, quite properly, disgusted with the whole business – we promptly discontinued the 'experiment'. Similarly, in my experience the most underused facility in Open University courses is the TV programmes – I think that students simply do not find watching TV a worthwhile learning activity, although they certainly find it entertaining.

Large 'small'-group teaching

'Small' groups become bigger. The very size of a group can inhibit its purpose. Discussion, informality and interchange all become more difficult, as more people crowd in. Assuming you have exhausted all the accommodation and timetabling options, such as splitting them up or alternating groups weekly, and you are still left with large groups, then there are a number of problems you face. Interpersonal distances must be reduced before free discussion can take place. You therefore need some sort of icebreaker, such as introducing neighbours. You certainly need to get them to learn each other's names. None of this is wasted time – it will pay dividends in later discussions. Such things as conduct of group sessions or seminar preparation could be included in the course handbook, in which you could also include space for the students to list the members of their group. Larger groups are more difficult to keep on track and you may need to adhere more strictly to a set agenda than you would normally like. Provided the room is large enough, you may be able to split the group into smaller subgroups, touring between these and finally bringing them together for a plenary session. For the large group, both you and the students will have to rethink your roles and strategy. You will need to act more as a consultant, a guide or a facilitator of independent learning. The students will need training if you are going to let them fend for themselves – again, this is not wasted time, these are valuable transferable skills you are teaching them. Habeshaw et al. (1992) provide many useful suggestions for dealing with large groups (see also Gibbs, 1992b).

Student consultation becomes more frequent

When your student numbers go up significantly, so do the numbers knocking on your door. You may then be forced to have fixed surgery times, to contain the increased disruptions, which may amount to an additional hour or more on your timetable – per course. You can also reduce the visits by providing as much information as the students need in the course handbook or in their notes. Obviously, the clearer you make your courseware, the fewer queries you will get. You could also avoid setting troublesome problems, or if you do set any, tell the students you will go through them in class, or issue solutions. If, after a couple of student visits, a pattern of queries emerges (it is usually one awkward question, or a mistake in a question), again deal with it in class or issue a solution. Accept that you can no longer give students the time you would like, and concentrate on the most deserving and needy cases.

Assessing large numbers of students

This can lead to significant problems. Some people advocate easing the burden of marking by using self-, peer- and group-assessment. There may be merit in this, but each of these requires recurrent training, organization and negotiation. Really these methods are probably best used to meet educational objectives, rather than as an efficiency measure. Another option is to reduce the amount of assessment. For example, you can reduce the amount of coursework, or even abandon it altogether and simply rely on a sessional exam. You could do some of the assessment by class tests, but this eats into contact time, and requires methods of avoiding cheating if students are crammed cheek by jowl in a crowded classroom (McGee, 1991). But all these are basically ways of reorganizing or limiting the amount of assessment. You can also consider ways of making the marking easier or more efficient. By using objective tests you can reduce the marking to a job for a secretary or computer. Although such tests assess limited educational objectives, they still allow you to reduce the really difficult marking of essay-type questions to more manageable proportions. This is essentially a form of front-ending the assessment, in which carefully planned setting of the assessment can reduce the labour of marking (Gibbs, 1992b).

Provided institutional regulations permit it you could also vary the way you examine students on the same course, giving them the choice of whether to have objective, essay, or oral tests, with a negotiated grading scheme. Most will opt for the objective test – the uncommitted majority. The keen students may opt for essay-type questions demonstrating greater understanding and attracting higher grades. The logic here is that most students are content to do moderately well, and if objective tests can provide greater certainty of a lower but adequate grade than an essay question might yield with lower certainty, then they will opt for the objective test. For similar reasons, you may be able to replace some assessment of some objectives with criterion-referenced assessment with a simple pass/fail grade. You will easily be able to spot the disadvantages of all these methods. One way or another, they are all tantamount to lowering the quality of the education and the standards achieved. As repeatedly pointed out by all the authors cited in this section, this is an inevitable consequence of teaching larger numbers of students, with reduced resources. All we can do as teachers is to mitigate the effects as best we can, resist, complain and inform students and the public of our concern.

If you do retain a significant element of coursework for large numbers of students then you will really need to get yourself organized if you are to keep any sort of social life. You can certainly afford to take greater advantage of objective tests, and self-, peer- and group-assessment for some continuous assessment. Also, by taking a very strong line on things like submission dates, tidiness and presentation, exacting penalties for nonconformance, you can reduce the amount of hassle these things bring. For essay questions requiring more careful marking, use prepared forms for entering your comments, illustrating how the marks are awarded (bless the word processor). You will find plenty more ideas in the references cited.

Evaluation

It is nice to end with some good news. Provided you can still find time for some evaluation, perhaps along the lines discussed at the end of Chapter Six (page 128), this need not necessarily be crucially dependent on the number of students. You only need to sample them for the purposes of feedback by questionnaire or interview, and even if you get returns from them all it is not onerous to skim through large numbers of evaluation forms. Indeed, because of the large numbers, the evidence and information you obtain will be more statistically reliable and therefore more useful. One warning, however. You will inevitably suffer from reflected discontent with the large class – student ratings of courses and lecturers with large numbers of students are invariably lower. McGee (1991) points to the evaluation item concerning availability to students. He goes out of his way to make himself available, yet always receives low ratings on this item. This simply reflects the students' perception of him as an unapproachable figure because of the sheer size of the class.

Chapter Eight

Teaching Issues of our Time

Where is university teaching heading?

For this concluding chapter, Phil Race suggested that I try to predict the range of duties of a teacher in higher education in the year 2020. I wouldn't know where to start, I'm afraid – but it does occur to me that the nature of the job will depend crucially on how the profession as an international community responds to some of the burning issues of today. So, in this last chapter, I would like to make some observations on a number of major current developments of global extent, which are important in university education and which our profession needs to address with some urgency and unity. These developments are:

- moves to measure and reward teaching;
- demands for greater efficiency;
- the overloading of courses and degree programmes;
- the impact of new technology;
- the nature of university management and governance.

I think that most university teachers, throughout the world, will have felt the impact of some, if not all, of these developments in recent years, often having to stand by, seemingly powerless, as they overwhelmed us. The profession's response to them has tended to be piecemeal rather than united and consistent, and reactive rather than proactive – usually to our cost. The representative bodies of academics at institutional, national and international level have a responsibility to promote debate and coordinate response to such developments, on behalf of their members – but conversely, we all have a responsibility to enter into informed discussion and think about the issues involved. With the rising pressures on us, and the preoccupation with mere survival, it is difficult to slow down for a careful, scholarly debate about the issues. But it is essential, if only to ensure that the teachers of 2020 will have a job worth having. Also, the run-down in education must eventually come to an end – or am I being naïve to believe that there is a limit to society's philistinism? Then it must be teachers who lead the way out of the educational recession. I don't know where university teaching is heading – but I know it is an important question. In this chapter I want to be a bit provocative about some of the issues involved.

Assessing and rewarding teaching

Many schemes for measuring and rewarding the quality of teaching have been mooted – reaching a crescendo in recent years. Perhaps the two key questions here are: (a) should it be done? and (b) how should it be done? If we cannot answer the second question, then the answer to the first must be 'no'. So, is it possible to obtain a reliable, valid and practical measure of teaching quality, as a basis for rewarding the deliverer? Let us be specific. In a department of 20 teachers, is it possible to rank them according to the quality of their teaching – if only crudely? Would such a ranking be robust enough to merit extra pay for the best and dismissal for the worst? Of course it is. You agree a panel of judges with the staff concerned; the panel gives impressionistic numerical scores in a given number of attributes (maybe planning, preparation, courseware, delivery, assessment, for example) and then plugs into some formula producing an overall ranking, with some means of dealing with ties. Provided you can obtain full agreement of the 20 candidates on the process (although some may find fault with the system after the results are announced!) this would seem to be a fair way to go about the exercise. I cannot imagine teachers agreeing to anything *less* equitable and democratic. The panel of judges would remove bias; the use of a range of attributes recognizes the multi-dimensional nature of teaching, the numerical scale could be simply poor, average, good and the ranking formula used could be demonstrably unbiased and fair.

Variations of such a scheme are already in place in some institutions and countries. But is it reliable, valid and practical? It is probably reliable, in the sense that if we choose a different panel of judges, there is a high probability that the results will be similar. Its validity depends on knowing the attributes of good teaching and being able to recognize and 'quantify' them *from limited evidence* and on the ability to summarize this in a valid ranking formula, weighting the different attributes appropriately. This is a very difficult problem, which I leave you to discuss with your colleagues. I do not know whether such validity can ever be guaranteed, but I am very doubtful that any current scheme provides it. Is it practical? Or, more important, is it cost-effective? Here I have serious doubts. The administration and execution of such a scheme could be very costly and recurrent, particularly if one assumes a reasonable turnover rate of staff in the department. Much more important, however, is the inevitable cost to morale and collegial cooperation which might follow the operation of such a scheme. As I have laboured throughout this book, teaching is a collegial, community enterprise (unlike research, which sometimes thrives on competition) and cannot be otherwise. Under such a scheme as that proposed above, natural academic altruism would, with the need for survival, soon wither. Staff would simply learn the rules, play the game and compete rather than cooperate. One would have to be absolutely certain that this would result in better teaching, and better trained students – and *significantly* better, to recover the recurrent costs. As an example, for you to interpret as you wish, some American surveys showed that after the introduction of student rating of instruction, the average grades of students increased significantly. Does this necessarily mean that teaching and learning had been improved? I have my doubts.

There are many schemes one could invent and who is to say that a suitable approach could not be found? For my part I am sceptical – but then I would be, wouldn't I? My main points here are that any proposal to assess and reward teaching must be debated thoroughly, democratically and extensively before implementation; it must be acceptable to the academic community and it must recognize that the invisible costs to the collegial fabric of teaching may far outweigh any gain in quality of teaching. We all want teaching to be first rate and to be valued, and the way to ensure this, it seems to me, is to first introduce and resource a carefully thought-out training scheme for university teaching and let the issue of assessment and reward develop naturally from that.

Demands for increased efficiency

Our trouble as university teachers is that too many of us (including me at times) have gone along with the myth that teaching is easy, off-the-cuff stuff and that research is the real thing – anybody can teach. It rarely occurs to us to compare the professional expertise and judgement required in teaching to that of say a lawyer, accountant, or doctor – of course, as a university teacher we may be any one of these but the teaching itself is often marginalized in our estimation. Since we ourselves underestimate the job of teaching, it is hardly surprising that those outside the profession, particularly those with influence and power, do too. As a result, every Tom, Dick and Harry feels they can expound on how to improve quality and efficiency in teaching. The truth is, in fact, with a highly interactive, human and community activity like teaching you *cannot* always improve efficiency – indeed, it is often very difficult to do so without unforeseen adverse effects. Teaching is a highly professional occupation, performed largely by able, sensible, committed people. To assume that they have not already optimized and regulated their own and the institutional performance is not only an insult (which, incidentally, most other professions would rebut vigorously) but is foolhardy and counterproductive. In order that non-practitioners appreciate that, it is essential that the profession itself recognizes and *publicizes* it. We must learn to exact our due credit in a world which is increasingly hostile to public services such as education.

But, the question still remains – can the efficiency of university teaching be improved and what costs to quality and standards would this imply? Again, this is a multi-dimensional problem, so we must be specific. Can our department of 20 teachers absorb another 10 per cent of students without lowering quality and standards (I know – you have already done so)? Well, of course, if they have found time to prepare their teaching profiles as required by the teaching quality assessment panel, and if they have increased their research output as required by their institution, then they have already increased their efficiency – but we are looking for something more on top of that. Chapter Seven looked at measures for increasing efficiency at institutional and individual level. Whether any of these is appropriate to our hypothetical department is for them to discuss (*not* for their head or chair to decree), but they must be fully aware of the costs which they all incur. Teaching classes which are 10 per cent larger increases marking, consultation and small-group teaching time. Combining disparate groups by modularization increases the workload on staff due to more difficult preparation and coping with great variability in background and motivation, while at the same time undermining the distinctiveness of the student's discipline. Use of information technology and computer-assisted learning is expensive in accommodation, hardware and training, and can compromise course objectives, as well as reducing students' contact with teachers. Use of part-time or underqualified staff has its limits and has problems of availability and accountability of such staff.

I don't doubt that our department will weigh the pros and cons of alternative teaching strategies and it may be that they can, in the end, point to real efficiency gains. All 20 staff would then presumably be happy with implementing these. But, again we must be aware of the hidden costs to morale and collegial structure, which such a process might incur – this must be set against any efficiency gain. This cost can only be minimized by a democratic, fully cooperative approach to the exercise, involving everyone and with the disadvantages of every proposal being examined objectively and in depth. It is fatal to impose efficiency measures by managerial edict – if you do, then you must add to your costs the difference between getting 100 per cent out of your staff and getting 40 per cent out of them.

The overloading of courses and programmes

Particularly if you are in a traditional subject area and have been teaching for 10 years or so, you will probably have noticed a significant increase in course content. Also, a number of extra topics may have crept into the degree programme – largely under the guise of transferable skills. It is natural, of course, that with the advancement of knowledge, the growth of technology and increased access, universities would want to introduce additional material into their programmes and courses. The same applies in school education. Indeed, it has always been the case that educational programmes expand and assimilate more material, but what has changed in the twentieth century is the *speed* at which this has taken place. Often, the time for careful deliberation about rationalizing that which is already taught to make way for new material has simply not been available and we have gone on cramming the stuff in until finally, in some subjects, the buttons are popping. The UK's Institute of Physics has finally grasped this nettle in university physics. The IOP recommended, among other things such as changes in teaching methods and a departure from lectures to small-group teaching, that the factual content of a single honours physics degree course should be reduced by a third. Not before time – now let us see this in other subjects (especially mathematics) and in the schools. Otherwise, I don't dare contemplate what our job will be like in 2020!

If you have experienced this burgeoning in course content (and possibly reduction in class contact too, at the same time), how have you responded? Many teachers have simply been forced to reduce depth in the course content, encouraging a surface or strategic approach to learning. Can this be right; and can it continue? No. We are entrusted with the best minds in our society – we cannot send them out with cookbooks and recipes. If they do not have a thorough, deep understanding of their subject, who will? And it is we, the teachers, who should ensure delivery of this depth of understanding and that means we cannot allow overloaded courses and programmes.

One of the reasons for setting detailed course objectives is that it gives you an idea of the time required to achieve these by way of a deep approach. If the time allocated is insufficient, then you do not compromise your approach – you either insist on increased time, or a reduced set of objectives. You are not doing the students any favours by piling in more and more material to accommodate your colleagues or accrediting institutions. If all physics lecturers had taken this stand 10 years ago, then I suspect that the IOP would have found little to worry about. I have been pleased to see recently a number of examples where teachers have finally decided enough is enough and have negotiated firmly for reduced content. I hope many more will do so. Just as important, I hope everyone will exert pressure on schools to reduce the content of their curricula.

The impact of new technology

There is, of course, nothing new about new technology. The printing press was once the last word in communication technology and there is no doubting its great impact on teaching and learning. It may be that the present wave of new technology may have a similar impact on teaching and learning. But how fast and how great an impact? I would like to see more caution exercised about the claims made for the benefit of such things as computer-assisted learning in education. There is a danger of overstating the case, with excessive claims leading to precipitate investment at great cost, financially and to the credibility of any real benefits there may be. Students, teachers and any educational system can only respond to changes and assimilate new developments at a limited rate and they must have time to absorb and assess the changes, while continuing to provide good education for the students. The pace of introduction of new technology must be driven by educational objectives and not by resource constraints, or the Stock Exchange.

If we examine exactly what it is that new information technology allows us to do, it is again uncertain whether the benefits are as great as is claimed. It allows faster and wider access and processing of information, but does this necessarily lead to more effective teaching and learning? The real core of teaching is in the explanation of the difficult, fundamental ideas, not in routine information transaction. Information technology may shift these difficult areas, and give us new fundamentals to struggle with – but the best way of tackling those will, I suspect, still be through the human teacher, not the TV or computer screen.

As for the oft-argued suggestion that computer screens may replace some functions of face-to-face teaching – well, what is replaced is not *teaching*. I don't think anything will replace face-to-face tuition. The advent of the printing press, radio and television has not reduced the need for live teaching. Indeed, the need for live teaching was probably increased by them. For example, the widespread use of the printing press eventually resulted in the need to teach the population to read – a job which still taxes the best of live teachers. Similarly, the computer's artificial presentation of information and knowledge is accompanied by a myriad questions for the learner, whose natural tendency will be to turn to human experts for clarification. As I have explained throughout this book, teaching and learning is, if anything, a matter of human interaction. I particularly notice this when I try to discuss difficult points with students over the telephone – I get frustrated because I know I could help them so much more easily if I had them in front of me, to watch their facial expressions, and their scribbles on paper. Mistaking a computer for a teacher is like mistaking a robot for a spouse (come to think of it ...).

The management and governance of universities

In many countries there has been a move towards introducing industrial and commercial personnel and practices into university management, with the claim that this will lead to more efficient and accountable performance. This is one issue on which I cannot vacillate. It is simply wrong, counter-productive and destructive to the efficient working of university govern-ance. University teaching is not about turning out a product or rendering a service to achieve maximum profit, which are the legitimate and respectable aims of a commercial enterprise. No chairman, no head of department, no one man or woman is capable of *directing* the activities of even a small group of academics – *leading* maybe, directing, no. No 'board' of senior people is capable of directing the activities of a group of academics, many of whom will be far better qualified for the purpose than senior staff. The governance of a university has to be by a democratic committee structure with broad representative membership and election by universal suffrage – it is not perfect, but it is the only way of getting the best out academics. There is no question of 'management' in the sense of 'to control' but only in the facilitation and coordination of everyone's best efforts. An academic leader leads by persuasion and personality or not at all; they should desire, and have, no power over conduct of teaching or research, and only that influence which they can engender by reasoned argument. No other way will work. That is the reason for tenure and academic freedom. The abolition of tenure in Britain has left many young staff on short-term contracts, the renewal of which may depend solely on the head of department. I have seen appalling treatment of such staff, who often feel unable to assert themselves and state their views in departmental meetings because of their dependence on an autocratic head of department. Also, their duties are often so tightly prescribed that they are not able to enter fully into the collegial and democratic activities of the university – such as service on academic boards and committees – they are effectively disenfranchised. What is more appalling is the lack of support they appear to get from their tenured 'colleagues' who tolerate such a situation.

In my view, there is no argument about the trend away from traditional, democratic governance of universities – it must be fought tooth and nail by every academic, everywhere, with the same ruthlessness with which it is imposed. This does not mean simply joining your professional association or union, but opposing the trend in every committee and at every possible opportunity; it means refusing to be 'managed' if this conflicts with your professional integrity; if you feel that the extra class you have been given by the head of department will result in a lower quality of education and an unreasonable imposition on your time, refuse to take it. The only obligation an academic has is to listen to the consensus of his colleagues. The job of an academic leader is to uncover and promote that consensus, and it is the responsibility of every academic to ensure that they do just that. The danger comes when we are too lazy, self-indulgent and witless to allow consensus to emerge, leaving the way open for autocratic 'management' to seize the initiative. I've seen enough of that to last me a lifetime.

Back to the classroom and sanity

If you have been in the teaching game long you will have wearied of the accountability, accountancy, efficiency, overladen courses, new developments and rampant, ignorant, philistine 'managers'. Where do we go for peace and solace in our job? I think the classroom and the students (preferably a small group). Bright, young (in heart – everyone who wants to learn is young, no matter what their age) people, full of vigour if you can stimulate it. Adaptable and unconcerned about the funding and organizational shock waves going through the system – except of course, for the deterioration in value of their own grants. In the classroom you can talk to them about mathematics, English, history, or whatever your subject is. Then you know why you became a teacher. If, after 10 minutes you can still see them as customers or products, then you are not cut out to be a teacher – find an easier job, or you will never stand the pace. On the other hand, if after 10 minutes the memories of the boring meetings and the ceaseless paperwork have floated away to oblivion, then keep at it – there may be a teacher in there somewhere. Enjoy your teaching and learning.

Appendix

As I have mentioned before, the object of this book is to stimulate thought on a whole range of teaching topics. The bibliography provides further reading in areas you are likely to be interested in. Books on teaching come in many types and I have deliberately chosen those for the bibliography to reflect this.

There are books which provide practical tips, perhaps best exemplified by the '53' books of Gibbs *et al* and the classic Teaching Tips of McKeachie, or McGee's 'survival kit'. Then there are those which leaven sound practical advice with some deeper philosophical or theoretical view of teaching, such as Eble, Lowman and Ramsden (there are many more to choose from – these are simply the ones I found most readable). Also, there are highly specialized books or monographs addressed at specific issues examined in depth, such as Ellis (1993). There are government and institutional reports and staff development material such as CVCP/USDU (1992). There are also many books containing case histories of educational developments, such as Gibbs and Jenkins (1992). But perhaps the last word in references is the excellent book by Menges and Mathis (1988). This gives commentary on some 600 key resources in higher education – a real treasure chest.

In addition to books, there are now a large number of journals devoted to all aspects of teaching in higher education. The following list scratches the surface, but should give you a good start:

Assessment and Evaluation in Higher Education (UK)
Canadian Journal of Higher Education (CN)
The Chronicle of Higher Education (US)
Higher Education (NE)
Higher Education Quarterly/SRHE (UK)
Higher Education Research and Development Journal (Australia)
Journal of Educational Psychology
Journal of Further and Higher Education (UK)
The Journal of Higher Education (India)
The New Academic
Studies in Higher Education (UK)
Times Higher Education Supplement

Many more such journals are listed in *The Serials Directory* (1992), Ebsco Publishing,

Birmingham, Alabama. For a concise list of journals devoted to teaching in specific subject areas, see Laurillard (1993).

There are, around the world, many institutions and organizations which specialize in promoting and disseminating teaching ideas in higher education (see, for example, Osborne (1991) or the UNESCO Directory of Educational Research Institutions (1986), prepared by the International Bureau of Education). Again, the following can only provide a starting point. If you are aware of important omissions, or errors in the information, please let me know.

UK

For general aspects of higher education teaching, promoted by publications, staff development courses, or consultation:

Oxford Centre for Staff Development Unit
Oxford Brookes University
Headington
Oxford
OX3 0BP

CVCP/Universities Staff Development Unit
Level Six
University House
Sheffield
SN10 2TN

Centre for Research in Learning and Instruction
University of Edinburgh
10/12 Buccleuch Place
Edinburgh
EH8 9JT

The Society for Research into Higher Education
344–345 Gray's Inn Road
London
WC1X 8BP

The SRHE publishes, with the Open University Press, monographs on all aspects of higher education. It also publishes the journals *Studies in Higher Education, Higher Education Quarterly, Research into Higher Education Abstracts* and the *SRHE News*.

Staff and Educational Development Association (SEDA)
Gala House
3 Raglan Road
Edgbaston
Birmingham
B15 7RA

SEDA, a result of the merger of SCED and the SRHE Staff Development Group, produces a wide range of publications and resources and organizes two annual conferences.

Centre for Higher Education Studies
Institute of Education
University of London

For CAL and other educational technology:

British Universities Film and Video Council (BUFVC)
55 Greek Street
London
W1V 5LR

Computers in Teaching Initiative Support Service
University of Oxford Computing Service
13 Banbury Road
Oxford
OX2 6NW

CTI subject areas are dotted around the country – for example, Mathematics and Statistics is based in the Faculty of Education, University of Birmingham.

Institute of Educational Technology
The Open University
Walton Hall
Milton Keynes
MK7 6AA

Other useful addresses include:

Quality in Higher Education Project
Baker Building
The University of Central England in Birmingham
Perry Barr
Birmingham
B42 2SU

which publishes reports arising from the QHE project, and

Higher Education for Capability Ltd
20 Queen Square
Leeds
LS2 8AP

which is a joint initiative with the RSA devoted to learner-managed education in the higher education context. It conducts workshops, conferences and publishes newsletters and a journal.

International Centre for Distance Learning (ICDL)
The Open University
Walton Hall
Milton Keynes
MK7 6AA

Australia

Centre for Educational Development and Academic Methods
Australia National University
GPO Box 4
Canberra City
ACT 2601
Australia

Centre for the Study of Higher Education
Institute of Education
University of Melbourne
Parkville
Victoria 3052
Australia

Educational Research and Development Unit (ERADU)
Royal Melbourne Institute of Technology
PO Box 2476
Melbourne
Victoria 3001
Australia

Higher Education Research and Development Society of Australasia (HERDSA)
Professional Development Centre
University of New South Wales
PO Box 1
Kensington 2033
Australia

Publishes *Higher Education Research and Development, HERDSA News*, annual conference proceedings, and *Green Guides* – texts and monographs on topical issues in higher education.

Tertiary Educational Institute (TEDI)
University of Queensland
Brisbane
Queensland 4072
Australia

Canada

Centre for University Teaching and Learning
McGill University
3700 McTavish Street
Montreal
Quebec
H3A 1Y2

Committee for the Improvement of Teaching and Learning
302E Students' Union Building
University of Alberta
Edmonton
Alberta
T6G 2J7

Educational Technology Department
Concordia University
1455 De Maisonneuve Boulevard West
Montreal
Quebec
H3G 1M8

Instructional Development Centre
McMaster University
General Sciences Building
Hamilton
Ontario
L8S 4K1

Open Learning Agency
300–475 West Georgia Street
Vancouver
V6B 4M9

USA

Academy for Educational Development (AED)
1255 23rd Street, NW
Washington DC
20037

American Educational Research Association (AERA)
12340 17th Street, NW
Washington DC
20036

This national centre publishes a journal, holds annual conferences and conducts research at all levels of higher education.

Center for Instructional Research and Curriculum Evaluation (CIRCE)
University of Illinois at Urbana/Champaign
1310 Sixth Street
Champaign
IL 61820

Center for Research on Learning and Teaching
University of Michigan
109 East Madison
Ann Arbor
MI 48109

Center for the Study of Evaluation (CSE)
Department of Education
UCLA
405 Hilgard Avenue
Los Angeles
CA 90024

Educational Technology Centre
University of California
Irvine
CA 92717

Instructional Technology Program
School of Education
Campus Box 106
PO Box 173364
Denver
CO 80217-3364

Learning Research and Development Centre (LRDC)
University of Pittsburgh
Pittsburgh
PA 15260

National Society for Performance and Instruction (NSPI)
1300L Street, NW
Suite 1250
Washington DC
20005

Office for Educational Research and Improvement (OERI)
US Department of Education
Information Services
Capital Place
555 New Jersey Avenue, NW
Washington DC
20208

Syracuse University Center for Instructional Development
111 Waverley Avenue
Suite 220
Syracuse NY
13244–2320

Bibliography

Abercrombie, M. L. J. (1974) *Aims and Techniques of Group Teaching*, Society for Research into Higher Education, London.

Andresen, L. W. (1988 2nd ed.) *Lecturing to Large Groups. A Guide to Doing it Less But Better*, Professional Development Centre, University of New South Wales, Sydney, and SCED, Birmingham.

Bales, R. F. (1950) *Interaction Process Analysis: A Method for the Study of Small Groups*, Addison-Wesley, Reading, Mass.

Barker, P. and Yeates, H. (1985) *Introducing Computer Assisted Learning*, Prentice Hall International, London.

Beard, R. M. and Bligh, D. A. (1971) *Research into Teaching Methods in Higher Education*, Society for Research into Higher Education, London.

Beard, R. M. and Hartley, J. (1984) *Teaching and Learning in Higher Education*, Harper & Row, London.

Bligh, D. A. (1974) *What's the Use of Lectures?* Penguin Education.

Bligh, D. A., Jacques, D. and Piper, D. W. (1981) *Seven Questions When Teaching Students*, Exeter University Teaching Services, Devon.

Bloom, B. S. (Ed.) (1956) *Taxonomy of Educational Objectives: Cognitive Domain*, Longmans, Green, London and New York.

Brenman, J., Goedegebuure, L. C. J., Shah, T., Weisterheijden, D. F. and Weusthof, P. J. M. (1992) *Towards a Methodology for Comparative Quality Assessment in European Higher Education*, Council for National Academic Awards, London, Centre for HE Policy Studies, The Netherlands, Hochschule-Information-Systems, Germany.

Brown, G. A. (1978) *Lecturing and Explaining*, Methuen, London.

Brown, G. A. and Atkins, M. (1988) *Effective Teaching in Higher Education*, Methuen, London.

Casey, F. (1985) *How to Study: a Practical Guide*, Macmillan Education, London.

Coate, L. E. (1990) *Implementing Total Quality Management in a University Setting*, Oregon State University.

CVCP (Committee of Vice Chancellors and Principals) (1992) *How to Do More With Less*, Occasional paper (29/1/92).

CVCP/USDU (Committee of Vice Chancellors and Principals/Universities' Staff Development Unit) (1992) *Effective Learning and Teaching in Higher Education. A* compendium of staff development resources consisting of a package of twelve modules, by various authors, in the area of active learning. USDU, Sheffield.

Deneef, A. L., Goodwin, C. D., and McCrate, E. S. (Eds), (1988) *The Academic's Handbook*, Duke University Press, Durham and London.

Department of Education and Science (1991) *Higher Education: A New Framework*, HMSO, London.

Devine, T. G. (1987 2nd ed.) *Teaching Study Skills: A Guide for Teachers*, Allyn and Bacon Inc., Mass.

Dressel, P. D. (1976) *Handbook of Academic Evaluation*, Jossey-Bass, San Francisco.

Eble, K. E. (1976) *The Craft of Teaching*, Jossey-Bass, San Francisco.

Ellington, H. and Race, P. (1993 2nd ed.) *Producing Teaching Materials*, Kogan Page, London.

Ellis, R. (1993) *Quality Assurance for University Teaching*, Society for Research into Higher Education and Open University Press, Bristol.

Entwistle, N. J. and Ramsden, P. (1983) *Understanding Student Learning*, Croom Helm, London.

Entwistle, N., Thompson, S. and Tait, H. (1992) *Guidelines for Promoting Effective Teaching in Higher Education*, Centre for Research on Learning and Instruction, University of Edinburgh, Edinburgh.

Ericksen, S. C. (1984) *The Essence of Good Teaching*, Jossey-Bass, San Francisco.

Gibbs, G. (1981) *Teaching Students to Learn: a Student Centred Approach*, Open University Press, Milton Keynes.

Gibbs, G. (1989) *Creating a Teaching Profile*, Technical and Educational Services, Bristol.

Gibbs, G. (1992a) *Improving the Quality of Student Learning*, Technical and Educational Services, Bristol.

Gibbs, G. (Ed.) (1992b) *Developing Teaching: Teaching More Students*, The Polytechnics and Colleges Funding Council.

Gibbs, G., Habeshaw, S. and Habeshaw, T. (1987) *53 Interesting Things to do in your Lectures*, Technical and Educational Services, Bristol.

Gibbs, G., Habeshaw, S. and Habeshaw, T. (1989 2nd ed.) *53 Interesting Ways to Appraise your Teaching*, Technical and Educational Services, Bristol.

Gibbs, G. and Haigh, M. (1983) *A Compendium of Course Evaluation Questionnaires*, SCEDSIP Occasional Paper, 17.

Gibbs, G. and Jenkins, A. (1992) *Teaching Large Classes in Higher Education*, Kogan Page, London.

Gould, S.J. (1991) *Wonderful Life*, Penguin Books.

Habeshaw, S., Gibbs, C. and Habeshaw, T. (1992) *53 Problems with Large Classes – Making the Best of a Bad Job*, Technical and Educational Services, Bristol.

Habeshaw, T. (1989) *Checking Out Your Course for Enterprise, Education and Improvement*, Bristol Polytechnic, Bristol.

Habeshaw, T., Habeshaw, S. and Gibbs, G. (1987) *53 Interesting Ways of Helping Your Students to Study*, Technical and Educational Services, Bristol.

Habeshaw, S., Habeshaw, T. and Gibbs, G. (1989) *53 Interesting Things to do in Your Seminars and Tutorials*, Technical and Educational Services, Bristol.

Harvey, L., Burrows, A. and Green, D. (1992) *Criteria of Quality*, QHE, The University of Central England in Birmingham, Birmingham.

Her Majesty's Inspectorate (1991) *Aspects of Education in the USA: Quality and its assurance in higher education*, HMSO, London.

Higher Education Council; National Board of Employment, Education and Training

(1992) *Higher Education: Achieving Quality*, Australian Government Publishing Service, Canberra.

Higher Education Funding Council for England (October 1992) *Quality Assessment.*

Hildebrand, M., Wilson, R. C. and Dienst, E. R. (1971) *Evaluating University Teaching*, Center for Research and Development in Higher Education, University of California, Berkeley.

Hills, P. and Gilbert, J. (Eds.) (1977) *Aspects of Educational Technology XI*, Kogan Page, London.

Jacques, D. (1991) *Learning in Groups*, Kogan Page, London.

Keller, F. S. and Sherman, J. G. (1974) *PSI: The Keller Plan Handbook*, W. A. Benjamin Inc, Menlo Park, California.

Kemp, J. E. (1980, 4th ed.) *Planning and Producing Audio Visual Materials*, Harper & Row, New York.

Laurillard, D. (1993) *Rethinking University Teaching: a Framework for the Effective Use of Educational Technology*, Routledge, London.

Lewis, R. (1981) *How to Write Self-Study Materials*, Council for Educational Technology, London.

Loder, C. (Ed.) (1990) *Quality Assurance and Accountability in Higher Education*, Kogan Page, London.

Lowman, J. (1984) *Mastering the Techniques of Teaching*, Jossey-Bass, San Francisco.

Lublin, J. (1987) *Conducting Tutorials*, Green Guide No. 3. HERDSA, Tertiary Education Research Centre, University of New South Wales, Kensington, Australia.

McGee, R. (1991 2nd ed.) *Teaching the Mass Class*, American Sociological Association, Washington.

McKeachie, W. J. (1978 7th ed.) *Teaching Tips: A Guidebook for the Beginning College Teacher*, D. C. Heath & Co., Lexington, Mass.

Maddox, H. (1988) *How to Study*, Pan Books, London.

Mann, R. D. *et al.* (1970) *The College Classroom: Conflict, Change, and Learning*, Wiley, New York.

Maxwell, M. (1980) *Improving Student Learning Skills*, Jossey-Bass, San Francisco.

Mehrens, W. A. and Lehmann, I. J. (1984) *Measurement and Evaluation in Education and Psychology*, Holt, Rinehart and Winston, New York.

Menges, R. J. and Mathis, B. C. (1988) *Key Resources on Teaching, Learning, Curriculum, and Faculty Development*, Jossey-Bass, San Francisco.

Meredeen, S. (1988) *Study for Survival and Success*, Paul Chapman, London.

Newble, D. and Cannon, R. (1991 2nd ed.) *A Handbook for Teachers in Universities and Colleges*, Kogan Page, London.

O'Neil, M. J. and Pennington, G. (1992) *Evaluating Teaching and Courses from an Active Learning Perspective*, CVCP/USDU, Sheffield.

Osborne, C. W. (Ed.) (1991) *International Yearbook of Educational and Training Technology 1991*, Kogan Page, London.

Partington, P. (Ed.) (1993) *Student Feedback – Context, Issues and Practice*, CVCP/USDU, Sheffield.

Percival, F. and Ellington, H. I. (1988) *A Handbook of Educational Technology*, Kogan Page, London.

Raahem, K., Wankowski, J. and Radford, J. (1991) *Helping Students to Learn: Teaching, Counselling, Research*, Society for Research into Higher Education and Open University Press.

Race, P. (1989) *The Open Learning Handbook*, Kogan Page, London.

Race, P. (1992) *53 Interesting Ways to Write Open Learning Materials*, Technical and Educational Services, Bristol.

Race, P. and Brown, S. (1993) *500 Tips for Tutors*, Kogan Page, London.

Ramsden, P. (1992) *Learning to Teach in Higher Education*, Routledge, London.

Ramsden, P. (Ed) (1988) *Improving Learning: New Perspectives*, Kogan Page, London.

Ramsden, P. and Dodds, A. (1989 2nd ed.) *Improving Teaching and Courses: A Guide to Evaluation*, Centre for the Study of Higher Education, The University of Melbourne, Parkville, Victoria 3052.

Rowntree, D. (1966) *Basically Branching*, Macdonald, London.

Rowntree, D. (1981) *Developing Courses for Students*, McGraw-Hill, Maidenhead.

Rowntree, D. (1987) *Assessing Students: How shall we know them?* Kogan Page, London.

Rowntree, D. (1990 2nd ed.) *Teaching through Self-Instruction: How to Develop Open Learning Materials*, Kogan Page, London.

Schön, D. A. (1983) *The Reflective Practitioner*, Temple Smith, London.

Shepherd, J. F. (1987 3rd ed.) *College Study Skills*, Houghton Mifflin, Boston.

Smith, M. and G. (1990) *A Study Skills Handbook*, Oxford University Press, Oxford

Startup, R. (1972) *Sociology – The Journal of the British Sociological Association*, 6, 2.

Stephenson, J. and Laycock, M. (Eds) (1993) *Using Learning Contracts in Higher Education*, Kogan Page, London.

Stephenson, J. and Weil, S. (1992) *Quality in Learning*, Kogan Page, London.

Weimer, M.G. (1987) *Teaching Large Classes Well*, Jossey-Bass, San Francisco.

Index